① ② ③

FORGET THE WEAPONS. USE YOUR HANDS. A ROUN
HOUSE IS DESIGNED TO LOOP AROUND OUTSIDE HIS AR
OF DEFENSE AND CATCH THE TARGET OFF-GUARD.

For optimum effect, throw a flurry of jabs first as a distraction.

If your neighbor pisses you
off, turn his hose on.
And don't turn it off.

JAB
JAB
JAB

HE PISSES YOU OFF
SO YOU MAKE HIM
COFFEE. AND LACE IT
WITH LAXATIVES

SEE THOSE ROUND COLORFUL THINGS ROLLING
AROUND THE TABLE? Pick up the nearest one.
Now wind up and throw your best fastball pitch.

GLASSJAW
anyone
susceptible
to
KNOCKOUT

✶ HOW TO ✶
KICK
— SOMEONE'S —
ASS

246 PRACTICAL
—but not always legal—
WAYS TO TAKE THE BASTARDS DOWN
⟨ E.R. SILVERMAN ⟩

▲adamsmedia
AVON, MASSACHUSETTS

Published by
Adams Media, a division of F+W Media, Inc.
57 Littlefield Street, Avon, MA 02322. U.S.A.
www.adamsmedia.com

ISBN 10: 1-60550-629-X
ISBN 13: 978-1-60550-629-6
eISBN 10: 1-4405-0715-5
eISBN 13: 978-1-4405-0715-1

Printed in the United States of America.

10 9 8 7 6 5 4 3 2 1

Library of Congress Cataloging-in-Publication Data
is available from the publisher.

This book is available at quantity discounts for bulk purchases.
For information, please call 1-800-289-0963.

DISCLAIMER

The contents of this book are intended solely for entertainment purposes. Due to possible injuries to yourself or others, you should not try to implement any of the ideas mentioned in the book.

ACKNOWLEDGMENTS

Thanks to Mike, a fly anywhere helicopter pilot, who gave me a crash course on how to maneuver an OH-58 during one of our operations. Just in case he became disabled in the air, he wanted the illusion of making it safely to the ground for medical aid, in which case the instructions were to find a very large, and very soft, cow pasture to drop it in, "cuz we may bounce a few times." It was only afterward that he explained to me that "helicopters don't really fly, they just beat the air into submission." I'm not sure if that was meant as encouragement, but it was an adrenaline-filled time in my life.

CONTENTS

INTRODUCTION · ix

LOCATION 1
THE BAR

1

LOCATION 2
ON THE ROAD
27

LOCATION 3
THE GYM
49

LOCATION 4
THE GAME
73

LOCATION 5
SOCIAL FUNCTIONS
89

LOCATION 6
THE HOME
107

LOCATION 7
ON VACATION
129

LOCATION 8
THE NEIGHBORHOOD
145

LOCATION 9
THE OFFICE
177

LOCATION 10
THE GREAT OUTDOORS
197

DEBRIEFING · 211

INTRODUCTION

There are plenty of reasons to want to kick some ass. Maybe your spouse ran away with your best friend and now you have fantasies of stuffing an angry cobra in his briefcase. Or perhaps that new coworker you helped out turned around and stole your ideas—securing himself a promotion while leaving you high and dry. Or maybe you have to go on the defensive and respond to some angry meathead who's trying to be a tough guy. Whatever the case may be, you have a lot of ass-kicking options.

Split up by location and then broken down by particular situations, you'll find more than 200 ways to respond to all the backstabbers and Neanderthals, a-holes and wannabes, punks and pricks who think they can get the better of you. Whether your attack needs to be physical or mental, immediate or planned out, you'll find some serious inspiration in the following pages.

As a former government agent, I've survived many hairy situations. In order to make it out in one piece, I needed to be prepared. You need to be prepared as well. You need to be physically and mentally tough enough to take on your Target and succeed in taking him down. Think you have what it takes? Reading this book is your first step to being prepared.

Now let's get a move on.

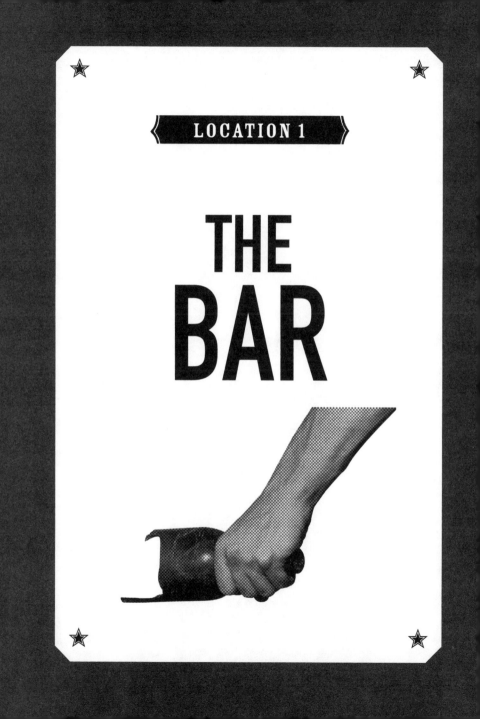

Can't a guy go out to a bar and get a drink in peace anymore? Seems like every time you drop into one of these places, some kind of ruckus starts up. Maybe you got bumped in the crowd and accidentally spilled your drink on the guy next to you—not really your fault. But hey, you don't even have to be part of a dispute to get swept up in a conflict. You could have been quietly sipping your favorite libation, checking out the local scenery, chatting with some friends, when—*Wham*—some idiot decides to make it personal.

Here are a few Ways to get out of the worst situations at your local watering hole. Sure beats lying on the floor looking up at the paramedics.

SCENARIO

YOU ACCIDENTALLY SPILL YOUR DRINK ON A GUY AND HE COMES CHARGING AT YOU. . . .

KARATE ROUNDHOUSE KICK Your nonkicking foot is positioned solidly on the floor for balance and your arms and hands are in the defensive position. Spin slightly on the ball of your nonkicking foot so your body is sideways to his. Plant that back heel into the floor. Your kicking leg is raised until it is parallel with the ground and your kicking foot is cocked back almost to your butt, knee pointed at opponent.

The kicking foot is snapped at the opponent's head or rib cage depending upon how high you can kick. Focus on the point of impact and immediately snap your leg back into the cocked position. This way, your opponent can't catch your leg. The velocity of the kick along with his own velocity should send him stumbling to the ground upon impact.

JUDO HIP THROW Use his momentum to pull him toward you and up on his toes. Slide your right arm around his waist as you pivot into him with your right foot leading. Rotate until your back is against his belly and your butt is against his groin. At this point you should be leaning slightly forward with knees bent. Your left hand continues pulling his right elbow forward, but now turn the pull into a downward direction. Your right arm and hips lead your opponent off the ground. Straighten your knees

KNOW THE LINGO

COUNTERMOVE

A defensive maneuver made in reaction to an opponent's move that is meant to weaken the opponent.

and your opponent gets launched over your right hip. Drop your body weight over your bent knees in a well-balanced stance as he hits the ground. This puts you close enough to his face to give a disabling strike, and it keeps him from pulling you down in a countermove, in case he's had any prior judo training.

KARATE PUNCH Okay, the guy's coming at you. Stand with your feet shoulder-width apart, knees slightly bent, and torso erect. Your left arm is forward with your fist turned palm down. Your right hand is cocked at your waist with your fist turned palm up. To punch, as your left hand is drawn back to your waist, it rotates so that fist is now palm up. At the exact same time, your right fist punches forward in a rotating motion so that fist finishes palm down with your big knuckles making impact on the Tar-get. Keep your shoulders square. There is no follow through on the punch like there is in boxing. Power comes from the rotation and snapping forward of the fist and from focusing your force on the point of impact. Quickly reverse the motions and punch with your left. Congratulations, you've just added a one-two punch to your arsenal.

WAITING AT THE BAR FOR A DRINK, SOME A-HOLE BEHIND YOU KEEPS PUSHING YOU. YOU TURN AROUND AND IT LOOKS LIKE HE'S ABOUT TO SWING. . . .

KARATE HAND JAB This form of the Hand Strike uses the tips of your stiffened fingers to jab the eyes or throat of the intended recipient much like a spear would strike, except that your fingertips become the blade of the spear and your forearm acts as the shaft of the spear. Just be sure

your fingers and wrist are locked tightly in place and are as stiff as a board at the time of impact. As a practical exercise, try jabbing your fingertips into a bucket of loose beans a few times to see if this works for you. Oh, and cut any long fingernails to prevent self-injury.

KARATE HAND STRIKE This is the old karate chop you saw in spy movies where the actor used the outside edge of his hand to "chop" the side of the neck of some unsuspecting guard on duty at the bad guy's secret hideout. The guard immediately fell down and went to sleep. Does it work? Let me put it this way: Black Belts break multiple boards and cement blocks with the edge of their hand all the time. Will it work for you? I don't know. Feel the outside edge of your hand. Any calluses? It takes time to build up this necessary toughness in your skin and bones. You sure don't want to be dancing around holding your broken hand while the bully takes advantage of your self-inflicted injury.

KARATE BACKHAND This is a technique where the recipient's subconscious immediately tells him, "Oh look, the wienie is leaving the field of battle." Yep, you have definitely turned your back on your opponent, normally an unwise decision, but this is only part of the movement. What you are actually doing is quickly spinning in a clockwise motion while slinging your right arm out to its full length just before the back of your right fist—and its two biggest knuckles—impacts on the side of his now unprotected face. If you are left-handed, then you spin counterclockwise to use the other fist. At this point, he recognizes his error, with maybe enough time for a quick "uh oh" just before he drifts off into the void. Fans of ultimate cage fighting have observed this particular technique in some of the matches. Works like a charm.

WALKING PAST THE POOL TABLE, SOME SHARK BLAMES YOU FOR HIS MISSED SHOT. HE'S COMING AT YOU WITH THE POOL CUE—AND HE DOESN'T LOOK HAPPY....

<u>KARATE FRONT SNAP KICK</u> Take a stance with most of your weight on your back leg. Your front foot barely rests on the floor and your body is upright and facing your opponent. To kick, your front leg rises so the top of your thigh is parallel, or higher, to the floor and your knee is bent with the back of your calf muscle touching the back of your thigh. The bottom of your kicking foot is parallel to the floor while your supporting foot stays flat on the floor. Now, quickly snap the kicking foot straight forward into his groin, chest, or face. Curl your toes so that the ball of the foot becomes the striking weapon. Snap your foot back to the ready position and you can provide more kicks if necessary. Maintaining your balance is very important during this movement.

KARATE BACK KICK Do an about-face and plant the nonkicking foot flat on the floor; tuck your elbows close into your body. Your forearms are positioned almost vertical so that both upper arms protect the sides of your rib cage, while your hands are in position to defend against blows aimed at your waist or above. As your opponent advances, your kicking leg cocks itself so that the kicking foot is now positioned about your opposite knee. Pivot slightly on the ball of your nonkicking foot until your body is sideways to his. Snap the kicking leg out so that the bottom of your heel hits his midsection. If your nonkicking foot is sufficiently planted, his forward momentum adds to the force of your kick. Quickly bring your kicking leg back to the cocked position.

PUT THE BOOTS TO HIM You're wearing a solid pair of boots and they should be good for something. First, throw a couple of punches to keep his eyes on your hands, and then, while he's distracted, use those boots to kick his shins, kneecaps, or higher if you can. And, if you get him on the ground, aim a couple more kicks to end the fight before you get hurt.

WARNING! *Do not* kick him in the vicinity of the head. It might make a good action scene in the movies, but in real life that kind of kick can be a killer. No sense in you going up for manslaughter.

SOME ADVICE . . .

Steel-toed boots are the best footgear for tap-dancing on someone's shins or kneecaps. The added weight and unyielding toe cap is almost as good as swinging a lead pipe when it comes to doing damage. The drawback is these boots can be expensive unless you have to buy them for your job anyway, plus they are heavier to walk around in than regular boots. Because of this extra weight, your legs will get tired faster in a fight, so end it early before you run out of breath. Also, don't try kicking above the waist because the extra weight slows you down and he may be able to catch your foot, which could be bad for your health.

SCENARIO

YOU AND YOUR DATE ARE CAUGHT IN THE MIDDLE OF A BRAWL AND THINGS ARE STARTING TO GET UGLY. NO ONE REALLY CARES WHO STARTED IT, AND NO ONE CARES WHO HE'S HITTING. LOOKS LIKE YOU'RE GOING TO HAVE TO GET PHYSICAL IN ORDER TO GET YOU AND, MORE IMPORTANTLY, YOUR DATE TO SAFETY. . . .

MUAY THAI KNEE If you remember to use your knees to good advantage, you can get through the crowd and out of the mess. Get a good grip on your Target's clothing up about the armpit or shoulder area, then quickly lift one knee and drive it into the bottom edge of his rib cage. It increases the force of the blow if you pull his body in the direction of your rising knee. After that, it's hard for him to breath with busted ribs. If you're really feeling frisky, leap up into the air while pulling down with both hands on the back of his neck and drive your knee into his face.

FIGHTING STYLE

Muay Thai: This is Thailand's sport of kick-boxing where the hands and feet are utilized as they are in karate, but the Muay Thai competitors also employ their knees in close-up fighting.

MUAY THAI ELBOW One of the methods of attack in Muay Thai is to throw a punch, immediately step in closer, and follow up the punch with an elbow in a diagonal slash or as an uppercut. The follow-up can also be an elbow delivered from the side and into the Target's face where the skin is close to the bone at the eyebrow. A cut here causes blood to flow over your opponent's eye, limiting his ability to see whatever else might be coming at him. And the sight of his own blood will cause a psychological reaction: the

Target will realize that he's been injured and should probably make a quick retreat off the battlefield.

MUAY THAI ANGLE KICK Very similar to the Round Kick used in karate, the Muay Thai Angle Kick is delivered to the exposed side of the opponent's torso or head, except it comes from what can be called a boxer's stance. If delivered by the fighter's right leg in an upward, angled strike to his left, he simultaneously rotates his arms and upper body to his right, which increases the force of the impact. Because of its intense power at point of delivery, many contact fighters of other martial arts employ this kick in their arsenal. In fact, it's used a lot in ultimate cage fighting matches.

SCENARIO

SOME GUYS JUST DON'T KNOW WHEN TO QUIT. SOME BIG, BURLY, DRUNK IDIOT STARTS PUSHING YOU AND INSULTING YOUR DATE. AS HE GOES TO GRAB AT HER . . . .

UPPERCUT For your Uppercut, step in close to your Target and drive your fist straight up under his guard and into the underside of his chin. The resulting sound of his lower teeth crashing into his upper teeth means you delivered this knockout punch correctly. If there is any power in your strike, the fight is over.

HOOK This maneuver employs the element of surprise. If you're right-handed, throw your Hook with your left hand. If you're left-handed, throw your Hook with your right hand. Hold your dominant hand up and swing with your nondominant hand. Turn your body with your punch and connect with your Target's face. Hopefully he's a glassjaw and will stay down.

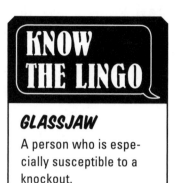

KNOW THE LINGO

GLASSJAW

A person who is especially susceptible to a knockout.

FIGHTING STYLE

Boxing: The ancient art of boxing has been around since the old Greeks and Romans decided they liked blood with their sports. The Romans, being more jaded, added metal to the leather hand wrappings in order to cause ultimate damage to their opponent. Today, boxers are required to wear padded leather gloves of a specific weight, and no metal, but don't kid yourself, professional boxers sometimes end up with brain damage from all the blows rocking their head.

JAB Fighters use this maneuver for two main purposes: distance and measurement. Thrown with the fighter's leading hand, the Jab flicks straight out from the shoulder toward the opponent's face. He usually steps back to avoid being hit, thus you keep him at a distance. If he stands his ground and ducks to avoid the punch then you try to step in with your opposite hand with an uppercut to his chin. If he fails to move back and also fails to duck, your jab will rock his world with whatever force is behind your fist. Jabs show you how your opponent reacts to your fighting style. Your brain then mentally calculates the distance one of your fists has to go in order to connect with his face. Your body moves forward accordingly to complete the job.

GO ON THE DEFENSIVE: Blocking the Punch

Most guys instinctively step back when they see a punch coming at them. But, what you should do is keep your feet in the same place and block the punch with your arm. For an incoming punch to the face or upper chest, karate fighters snap their forearm up and block the blow with the inside edge of the forearm. For an incoming punch to the solar plexus or abdomen, they snap their arm down and outward to block with the outside edge of their forearm. Use your left forearm to block his right-hand punch and vice versa. By blocking and not retreating, you are now close enough to your attacker for you to counterattack with a punch or kick before he has time to withdraw out of range.

Muay Thai fighters have a different philosophy on countering their opponent's punches. When their opponent throws a punch, instead of using a rigid block, they merely tap the approaching hand away. Using their left hand against the opponent's right-hand punch and vice versa, the Muay Thai fighter taps the back of his opponent's punching hand, which pushes the punch away and to the inside. By using just enough strength to deflect the attempted strike and no more, the Muay Thai fighter saves his energy for the long run in order to outlast his opponent. This method obviously takes lots of practice for your brain to auto-matically compute the proper distance to deflect the blow.

SCENARIO

NEXT! AFTER SEEING YOU TAKE OUT HIS BUDDY, HIS EVEN BIGGER, NASTIER, EVEN DRUNKER FRIEND DECIDES HE WANTS A PIECE OF YOU. TAKE HIM DOWN. . . .

JUDO FOOT SWEEP You grab your Target's right elbow with your left hand and pull down and out while using your right hand to pull his left shoulder up to his right (your left) and push backward. His body becomes a vertical wheel that you are rotating counterclockwise. The inside of your left foot then sweeps across the floor at ankle height and knocks his right leg out from under him. Bang, he's on his back looking up at you.

FIGHTING STYLE

Judo: This Olympic sport entails each contestant grasping his opponent's clothing with one hand at the elbow and the other near his collarbone. Using various techniques, the fighters throw their opponent to the mat. Fine for a sport, but in a street fight, your opponent will probably punch you out rather than dance around a mat. However, if you end up in a clinch situation here are some judo throws that may help.

JUDO LEG SWEEP The Leg Sweep also utilizes the fact that most of his weight is on one foot. To sweep his right leg out from under him, you pull down and out on his elbow with your left hand, while simultaneously pulling up to his right and pushing backward with your right hand, which is grasping his shirt on his left shoulder. His weight should now be mainly on his right leg. You step into him with your right leg to hook the inside of your right knee behind the inside of his right knee. Yanking your bent right leg strongly back toward yourself removes the main leg supporting his body, and once again he ends up on his back staring at the ceiling. Both the Foot Sweep and the Leg Sweep can be done from either side by reversing the directions for hands and feet.

JUDO MAT WORK—OR NOT Okay, you used one of these judo throws and your opponent is flat on his back. Now what? Well, Bud, if this is a bar brawl, you'd best be pounding fists into his face while you have the advantage, or else stand up and put the boots to him; otherwise you could be in for a long wrestling match. In judo competition, they call the physical workout after the throw mat work. And if you've had judo training then you've probably learned all about takedowns, reversals, holds, pressure on the joints, and various choke positions. But then like I said earlier, judo is a sport with rules, plus they have a referee. When's the last time you saw a referee for a bar fight? Do what's necessary for you to be able to walk away at the end.

SOME ADVICE . . .

When using techniques from any of the martial arts or other fighting methods, one of the key items to remember is balance. Your center of balance is your stomach, which should always be centered over whatever stance your feet and legs have assumed. Lean the top of your torso very far in any direction and you are easy to topple, while your ability to utilize any disabling techniques becomes severely diminished. For example, take a barstool: on all four legs, it is stable; tilted on any two legs, it becomes unstable; tilted onto one leg, it's easy to push over. So, you need to maintain your balance while pushing, pulling, leaning, or otherwise maneuvering the other person into having his body weight out of balance. Then you can handle him any way you want.

SCENARIO

YOU DIDN'T START IT, BUT SOME NEANDERTHAL KNUCKLE-DRAGGER PLANS ON FINISHING IT. THIS GUY LOOKS LIKE HE'S ABOUT TO SERIOUSLY THROW DOWN. AND HE MIGHT EVEN HAVE A WEAPON ON HIM. . . .

KNUCKLES MADE OF BRASS In the old Roman Coliseum, boxing competitor's hands were wrapped in leather and then covered with bits of metal. A more modern-day inventor poured hot metal into a mold shaped to fit all four fingers, much like four large rings welded together, with a supporting bar to fit into the palm of the hand. The most popular metal knuckles at the beginning were made

of brass, hence the name. Mine are made of iron alloy and have been chromed for psychological effect. You should also know that brass knuckles are difficult to find unless you're a member of one of the mafias, an old-style commando group, or you've visited certain third-world countries.

WARNING! At some time, you've probably thought about carrying them, but don't, unless you keep a lawyer and bail bondsman on retainer. Brass knuckles are illegal in most states.

WITH THIS RING... For those who don't want to get busted for carrying a set of brass knuckles, their answer is to wear one or more massive rings on each hand. These rings are made of heavy metal and generally have sharp edges all around the top side in order to cut the opponent's skin. These types of guys like to get up close and personal when they fight. The prison inmate's version of this same method involves holding sharp objects between the fingers or knuckles of their tightly closed fist so that the point or cutting edge slashes the opponent's face.

GIMME A BEER In the movies, our hero merely bangs his beer bottle against the bar and presto, a sharp weapon. Have you looked at the construction of a beer bottle lately? Most have thick bottoms and the rest is thin glass. There's no guarantee where that thin glass will break or in how many pieces. You could end up holding the stub of the bottle neck with your bleeding palm curled around sharp glass. So if a beer bottle is your weapon, leave the bottom on. If you insist on breaking the bottle against the bar for psychological effect, then wrap a bar towel around your hand first.

There Was This One Time . . .

Sometimes using psychological warfare lets your Target kick his own ass. While partying with the Canadian Mounties, I realized they were filling our drink glasses more frequently than their own. Evidently, it was their way of maintaining their image of legendary drinking prowess. To counter that, I made quiet arrangements with a friendly waitress to have two out of three drinks destined for our agents to be nonalcoholic but to resemble whatever alcohol had been ordered. For example, water shots instead of vodka shots. To avoid suspicion, I occasionally asked one of the Mounties to taste my real drink, claiming I wasn't sure it was the call brand I'd ordered. Naturally, it was, and this little ploy helped us put them under the table. Use this trick in conjunction with some of the following Ways.

GO ON THE DEFENSIVE: Getting Back Up

And if things go wrong in a hurry—either he connected with a punch or pushed you down—you may end up on your back. That's not always a bad position to be in *temporarily*. On your back, you can keep your legs cocked for kicking and use your hands to pivot your body on the floor so you're always facing him. Don't let him grab your foot. If he is overconfident and moves too close, kick his shin, groin, or chin. When he is distracted, move into a sitting position with your weight supported on your right hand to the rear and your left leg crossed over your bent right knee with your left hand resting on your left knee. Leap up and back into a defensive stance. Keep your head back and out of his reach, with your eyes always on him and what he's doing. Now you're up and ready.

SCENARIO

SOME OBNOXIOUS D-BAG TAKES A SEAT NEXT TO YOU AT THE BAR. BETWEEN YAKKING ON HIS IPHONE TALKING ABOUT HOW LAME THE PLACE IS AND HOW AWESOME HE IS, HITTING SHAMELESSLY ON THE NICE BARTENDER, AND JUST GENERALLY BEING A WASTE OF OXYGEN, HE'S REALLY STARTING TO PISS YOU OFF. . . .

THE CHEAPSKATE You're sitting at the bar close to your Target. You're each paying cash on separate drink tabs. Your Target calculates the amount for a tip and tosses the cash onto the bar before he walks away. You look around. No one is paying attention. You surreptitiously scoop up most of his tip and add it to the twenty percent tip you're giving. Leave only a couple of quarters behind for his tip. The bartender perceives you as a very generous customer and you receive great service in the future. Your Target is perceived as a cheapskate and finds strange objects in his future drinks. Repeat process.

IT'S CRUEL TO BE KIND Look around until you locate the least attractive female in the joint. Next, find a busy waitress, give her money, and tell the waitress to take that female a drink. Also point out the Target, instructing the waitress to say this drink is from *him* and he would like to meet the female. Ugly will soon be at his side. Now he's got a problem. If he's crude and rude, those around him will think badly of him, and if he's polite, then he has company for as long as he stays there. Don't laugh so loud that he figures out you're the one who set him up.

LAST CALL You've finally had enough listening to him shout into his phone. Who's he trying to impress, or has the cell phone become part of his obsessive personality? When he's occupied with something else and has to lay the phone down for a while, soak the phone in a cola drink. The cola corrodes metal parts, causes short circuits, and leaves everything inside as a sticky mess. You ever see what some cola drinks do to a penny? Well, that's what he's looking at. Wipe off the sticky outside to leave no trace of what happened. Oh yeah, turn off the phone before dunking.

SCENARIO

YOU'RE ON THE POOL TABLE WITH A COUPLE FRIENDS HAVING A FUN TIME WHEN THE GUY AT THE TABLE NEXT TO YOU JUST WON'T LEAVE YOU ALONE. HE'S TRYING TO TRIP YOU WITH HIS STICK, BACKING INTO YOU WHEN YOU'RE SHOOTING, AND JUST BEING AN ASSHOLE IN GENERAL. IT'S TIME HE LEARNED A LESSON. . . .

ON CUE You may have to skip a better shot in order to line this one up correctly. With a long and sudden drawback on your pool stick, go as far back as needed with the weighted end. Of course your back was turned to him, so you had no idea he was in the drawback line of fire. Since the wrong end of the cue just hit the wrong ball, be a gentleman and help him catch his breath.

ROUNDHOUSE A Roundhouse is designed to loop around to the outside of your Target's face. Throw a flurry of jabs first as a distraction. This brings his defensive hands more to the inside, thus allowing more room to loop a punch around them, plus as he brings his guard in, his own fists now limit his ability to see anything rocketing in from the side. By the time he sees your Round-house coming, it's too late to do anything about it except roll with the punch. Since your opponent will be throwing punches of his own, you better have your own program of bob-and-weave. One problem of learning the manly art of pugilism is that by the time you get the hang of it, you've already been thumped several times by better fighters.

YOU SAID WHAT? Rather than go the physical route, let someone else. Look for the biggest group of thugs in the bar, and insult them in your opponent's name while he's in the bathroom. Be subtle in how you do it. For example, just happen to mention, with all due respect of course, that the guy who just went into the restroom called them all something derogatory as he walked

by. The thing about a gang member is that they never want to come off as weak in front of another member. So while a simple insult may not instigate an individual standing alone into action, being insulted in front of a group will likely spur him into action. The other thing about gangs is that members seldom fight opponents one on one; it's more of a "everybody jumps in" thing. That guy doesn't know who he just messed with.

LOCATION 2

ON THE ROAD

Wherever you travel you may run into trouble, but there are bound to be objects at hand you can use to defend yourself. They may exist naturally in whatever environment you find yourself, or perhaps it is something you happen to carry in your car for times like these. In any case, you weren't looking for a fight and you didn't start the fight, but you want to end it before you get hurt. The basic rule of thumb is: "It's better to be tried by twelve than carried by six." And, if necessary later, the key words are: "Sir, I was afraid for my life." This doesn't mean the law won't give you trouble, but hey, you're alive and it improves your chances. So, to be on the safe side, maybe you pack a little defense inside your ride.

SCENARIO

AT A FOUR-WAY STOP YOU HAVE THE RIGHT OF WAY, BUT INSTEAD SOME JERK T-BONES YOU AS YOU GO THROUGH THE INTERSECTION. HE COMES BARRELING OUT OF HIS CAR WITH A PIPE. BETTER SEE WHAT YOU HAVE IN YOUR TRUNK—FAST. . . .

YOUR BASIC WOODEN SLUGGER Obviously, you have it there because you're meeting friends for a game. Not because you were planning on bashing someone's windshield in. (For credibility, you should also have a ball and glove in plain sight.) The wooden bat, long a favorite with loan sharks, does a lot of damage. However, if you keep up with sports, you know that a good maple bat needs to hit its object directly on the logo or sweet spot to work best. There have been several recent incidents of batters, other players, and umpires being severely cut by flying pieces of broken bats. So remember, if you inadvertently hit something hard, other than your intended Target, you may end up holding a very large toothpick.

A GOOD LEVER CAN MOVE THE EARTH Anytime someone has a heavy object to move, such as a fair-sized rock, or needs to pry two objects apart, such as a crushed fender off the front tire so he can drive a wrecked car, he immediately thinks about the crowbar. Crowbars come in assorted lengths and thicknesses. They usually have a wide, split hook at one end for extracting large nails from wood and an oversized flat blade on the other end for moving objects or prying them apart. I think your imagination can now take over, so that's enough said about this tool other than it rides nicely in a car trunk or truck bed.

IF YOU WERE A CARPENTER ... The common piece of lumber found at construction sites is the two-by-four. It's also found in backyards, garages, and scrap lumber piles. And, while it is a handy size to fit your hands, just keep in mind that any two-by-four over three feet long becomes unwieldy when swinging it as a weapon. Plus, they tend to crack in the middle when they make hard contact with a solid object. So, if a two-by-four is your only weapon of defense, use it wisely and go for the softer parts of your opponent—the nose, neck, or ribs—or use it as a blunt lance to jab at the face, throat, or groin. As far as lugging one around as a personal weapon, that choice sucks. It's tough to conceal one on your person, but it looks normal in the back of a pickup truck.

SCENARIO

TURN SIGNAL ON, YOU WERE JUST ABOUT TO PULL INTO A SPOT OF AN EXTREMELY CROWDED MALL LOT WHEN THIS JACKASS TEARS IN FROM THE OPPOSITE DIRECTION. DESPITE YOUR HONKING (AND YELLING AND SWEARING), HE GIVES YOU THE FINGER AND WALKS INSIDE. DON'T BOTHER GETTING PHYSICAL—GET EVEN. . . .

MECHANICS LOVE YOU Swing by the nearest coffee shop and pick up a handful of those little sugar packets. Then go find his car. Open up the access door leading to his gas cap. Unscrew the cap and place it on the cement down by his rear tire where it can be easily seen. Tear the tops off the sugar packets. Generously pour some of the sugar onto the bottom of the receptacle around the tube where he fills his gas tank. Leave one of the sugar bags lying near the pile of white crystals. Place the other empty sugar packets around the gas cap on the ground. He will assume his gas tank has been sugared, which will cost him in mechanic fees or personal labor to drain the tank of perfectly good gas.

THE POTATO GUN Kneel down at the rear of his vehicle and insert a fresh potato into the tail pipe opening, one in each if he has dual exhaust. Jam the spud all the way in until it seals the diameter of the pipe. Park about a block away to watch. His running car engine gradually builds up pressure as the burning gases try to escape through the exhaust pipes. When the pressure becomes strong enough, either the engine will sputter and die or it will fire the vegetable several yards down the street. You have just created a new version of the potato gun.

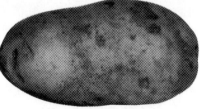

THE MAGIC ACT If you're *really* resourceful, try this out. Using some power tools—and the help of some equally able-bodied friends—quickly dismantle his vehicle and move all to the top of a nearby building or structure. Now, rebuild the entire vehicle. Let him figure out how to remove it. This is an old college prank usually done by mechanical or engineering students. Remember though: It's ready, set, *go*, the clock is ticking.

SCENARIO

SEE SOMEONE DING YOUR BEST BUDDY'S CAR AND THEN DRIVE AWAY? DON'T JUST TAKE DOWN THE GUY'S PLATE. USE IT FOR SOME VIGILANTE VENGEANCE. . . .

THE DOPPELGANGER EFFECT Write down your Target's license plate number. Then, back in your workshop, use your own license plate as a template to cut a piece of sheet metal to the same size. Drill mounting holes and paint the plate to match his in color, design, and numbers. Rent a vehicle resembling his in year, model, and color. Attach the fake plate to your rented vehicle and run a few tollgates that only take exact change and have

KNOW THE LINGO

DOPPELGANGER
A lookalike.

surveillance cameras with no people as toll takers. Wear a hat or otherwise disguise your appearance. When the surveillance photos get developed law enforcement will read the license plate numbers and send him a ticket for a hefty fine. How can he dispute the photo?

THE SWITCH If your Target has two vehicles, that means he has two sets of license plates. Find a quiet time to switch each set of plates to the opposite vehicle. Since most people don't memorize their license plates, he'll never know the difference. But when a cop stops him for speeding or some other traffic offense and runs the license numbers, the numbers don't come back to that vehicle. At the best for him, he looks like a dumb ass to local law enforcement. At the worst, he gets another ticket from an overworked policeman who doesn't see the humor in the situation. As for you, you haven't stolen anything—he still has all his property.

THE *BIG* SWITCH Okay, so you're a lot more unhappy with your antagonist than to merely switch his own license plates between two vehicles belonging to him. You want to take it a step further where it's hard for him to explain to the law why he has someone else's plate instead of his own. Now you need some privacy and his car needs to be parked beside someone else's vehicle. With your screwdriver or ratchet set, swap his license plates with those belonging to a stranger. Don't get caught by the cops, who will think you're stealing cars, or by the owner of either vehicle who might get nasty about you messing around with their property. Watch out for parking-lot surveillance cameras.

SCENARIO

THAT A-HOLE DID IT AGAIN! HE PARKED HIS CAR JUST ENOUGH IN FRONT OF YOUR DRIVEWAY SO THAT YOU HAVE TO MANEUVER AROUND IT AND RUIN YOUR GRASS. TIME TO SHOW HIM WHOSE CURB HE'S PARKING IN FRONT OF. . . .

IT LINGERS LONG On a hot day, catch his car with the windows rolled down a little to keep hot air from building up on the inside. Take your leftover carton of milk from lunch, and pour the white liquid through the space left by the low-ered window. You have two options: keep the milk off the window glass in order not to give away the future surprise, or let the milk dribble down the inside of the window glass and therefore into the interior of the door where it will be more difficult to clean up. Either way, the hot temperature quickly turns it sour forever.

THE FREAKY LEAK Periodically, at random times, let a few pounds of air out of the same tire on his vehicle. He will fill the tire several times before he suspects it has a slow leak somewhere and takes it to a mechanic for testing. You have now created two problems. First, it is difficult these days to find an air pump at a gas station for him to refill the tire himself, and if he does, they usually want a few quarters for a few pounds of air. Seems even air isn't free anymore. And secondly, when his mechanic finds nothing wrong with

the tire, the car owner and the mechanic will soon be at odds when the loss of air continues. Have a nice day.

PAINTING WITH TIRES Fill four sealable plastic bags with bright yellow paint, or each of the four bags with a different color paint depending upon your artistic sense. When the Target finally moves his car, follow him until he parks in his own driveway. Place the bags behind each tire of your Target's vehicle. Be sure the bags are out of sight from whichever direction he approaches his vehicle to open the door. By the time he backs out of his driveway, the artwork is already put in motion. And each

rotation of the tires adds to the artistic canvas. Remember, art is in the eye of the beholder. Not everyone takes the same pleasure in a painting.

YOUR JERK OF A "FRIEND" CONS YOU INTO DRIVING, YET AGAIN, WHEN YOU GO OUT ON THE TOWN TOGETHER. SOMEHOW, HE ALWAYS HAS A REASON OR EXCUSE WHY HE CAN'T BE THE DESIGNATED DRIVER. MAKE THIS THE LAST TIME HE TAKES ADVANTAGE OF YOU. . . .

SMELLS FISHY TO ME Make a copy of his car keys (unless you can find another way into the trunk). Next, wait for an event when his car will sit out for a couple of days in the heat. When the time is right, you avail yourself of a nice meal of seafood—shrimp, fish, crab legs, makes no difference. Have some left over when you're finished eating. Leave these leftovers out in the sun for a few hours if you have enough time. Bag everything up. Now scatter these leftovers throughout the trunk of his car. Neighborhood cats will follow him everywhere.

CHEESE IT Pick a nice, smelly cheese such as limburger. You now have two choices. You can place a large portion of this cheese on top of his engine and when the engine block heats up it will melt the cheese right onto the metal and therefore smell for weeks every time the motor runs. Or, to make it more difficult to locate the source of the odor, you can tape the cheese to the top side of his muffler. This second option has the advantage of you not having to gain access to the vehicle's interior in order to open the hood, plus the muffler heats up slower than the engine block, so there's a delayed smell reaction.

LARDY, WHAT A MESS Your Target caught a late flight back and his vehicle is waiting for him in the airport parking lot. He's tired and just wants to get home. Claiming his luggage, he takes the long walk out to his car. Approaching the vehicle, he notices something is wrong. There's a thick white substance smeared over all his windows. He runs his finger through the gooey mess. Lard. Now he has to trudge back to the terminal to find a restroom where he can steal paper towels to clean up his windows good enough to find his way to a car wash. Otherwise, his driving vision is like looking through wax paper. Remember to watch out for surveillance cameras in the lot.

WALKING TO YOUR CAR AFTER A WORKOUT YOU WATCH SOMEONE SCRATCH YOUR CAR AND SPEED AWAY. AFTER STAKING OUT THE GYM'S LOT YOU SPOT THE GUY WHO MESSED UP YOUR RIDE. LET HIM GO IN FOR A WORKOUT, THEN TAKE REVENGE. . . .

UNBALANCED Catch the Target's car when it's unoccupied. Stroll by to ensure no one's watching, and use a tire iron or large screwdriver to loosen one hubcap at the bottom of one of the wheels on the passenger's side so that it is not immediately noticeable to the driver. Sooner or later while driving around, this hubcap will come off and disappear into the roadside scenery. His ride will then acquire an uncool look while motoring around town with one hubcap missing, plus the Target will find it difficult and costly to locate and purchase a replacement for his one missing part. Repeat as necessary.

NO TRACTION Jack up the rear end of your Target's car and place cement blocks or other strong material underneath the vehicle frame until the rear tires are just barely off the ground after the jack is lowered. When the Target

starts up his car and shifts the transmission into gear, the rear wheels rotate, but the vehicle goes nowhere. His first reaction will be one of confusion, followed by the impression that either his transmission is slipping or his rear end has busted something internally. Depending upon how slow his mind is, he may just sit there for a while spinning his wheels.

WARNING! This will only work for two-wheel drive vehicles.

ONLY FLAT ON ONE SIDE   When the Target's vehicle is away from the convenience of his residence or place of employment, depress the valve stem on each tire to let most of the air out. Not so bad—they're only flat. But wait, you're not through yet. Take out your tube of superglue and apply it to each valve stem cap. Screw the caps back onto the stems and depart the area. Somebody can show up with an air compressor to inflate the tires, but they still have to find a way to get the valve stems open in order to put air in the tires.

DID THAT GUY JUST FLIP YOU OFF? TAIL HIS ASS AND WAIT UNTIL HE PARKS. THEN HAVE SOME FUN WHILE HE'S AWAY FROM HIS CAR. . . .

HELP ME To draw the wrong type of attention to your Target, use a large marking pen in a bright color on a thin piece of pliable cardboard to create a handwritten sign that says in large letters: *Help! Kidnapped. Can't Breathe.* Print the letters and words so that they appear to have been written in the dark under adverse conditions. Walk past the rear of his vehicle and insert the sign face up partially under the trunk lid. Make the sign look like it was pushed out from inside the trunk. Some passerby will start the ball rolling. Make sure there are no surveillance cameras for security to check later.

OFFICER, I THINK THERE'S A BODY You're driving by a parking lot and there his car is, sitting unattended. Of course, you're prepared. In a small ice chest, you have a squeeze bottle filled with chicken blood or the blood of some other deceased animal being processed for food. As you walk by the rear of his car, you empty the liquid contents of the squeeze bottle at the bottom of his

trunk lid down over the rear bumper, forming a pool of red onto the asphalt below the trunk. Conceal the squeeze bottle in a shopping bag. If none of the passing shoppers notice the pool of blood, you may have to point their attention in that direction before you leave the scene to watch from a distance.

THE MYSTERIOUS DRIP You know those small plastic cups used for dunking your French fries in ketchup? Well, the next time you're in a fast-food restaurant, stock up on a dozen. Fill one of these cups, or more, with transmission fluid. Slide yourself partway under your Target's car in his driveway and place the cup(s) on top of the transmission case. The next time your Target drives his car, the cups will slosh red fluid onto the transmission where it will run down to the

underside and drip off the bottom. Repeat periodically. He'll wonder where the leak is in his transmission, but mechanics will find no problem, unless they decide to charge him for a leak that doesn't exist.

SOMEBODY SERIOUSLY MESSING WITH YOUR PERSONAL BUSINESS? TEACH HIM TO MIND HIS OWN BEESWAX BY GETTING INVOLVED IN HIS. . . .

<u>**THE STING**</u> Wasps are usually found in papier-mâché-type nests under the eaves of a roof, or underneath a wooden deck. These nests are best gathered at night when wasps are more docile. Slide a bag up around the nest, detach it from its anchoring stem, and close the bag. Wear protective clothing in case a few unhappy wasps get outside the nest. No sense getting yourself stung. Now, place the nest inside the Target's car.

WARNING! Make sure your Target is not allergic to wasp stings. Remember, your goal is aggravation, not anaphylactic shock and charges of negligent homicide.

HE'S CHEATING ON ME Acquire some slinky feminine underwear, and no, I don't care how you get it, but if it's new, then wash it a few times so it at least appears to belong to someone. Place the underwear in glove box of his car, which his significant other will likely open as the passenger before he does. If his significant other is a large woman, make the lingerie a petite size, and vice versa.

YOU'RE BOOTED, BUDDY Chances are the Target is the type of slime to pull in front of a fire hydrant or park without paying the meter. Tail him until he gets caught. It doesn't matter what the violation is. The main thing is a violation has occurred and it happened to your Target. What do you do? Naturally, you take the ticket from under the windshield wiper and throw it away. He doesn't know about the ticket, and therefore he doesn't pay it. If this is his first offense, he'll get an additional fine. But if he has multiple outstanding citations, the next time police find his car, it gets booted or towed. And, if he's driving the car and gets stopped by the law, he stands to get cuffed and stuffed into the back of a cruiser.

SCENARIO

SOME GUY'S SPEEDING UP AND DOWN YOUR STREET, TERRORIZING YOUR NEIGHBORHOOD. TIME TO TAKE YOUR OWN RIDE FOR A SPIN AND TRACK HIM DOWN. ONCE YOU FIND HIM . . . .

FALSE REPORT Find your Target's vehicle with the passenger side window rolled down (or lower it yourself). As a preliminary measure to this endeavor, you've swept up and bagged broken glass from any area parking lot where cars are regularly broken into and looted. Spread the broken glass from the accident cleanup both onto the front seat of your Target's car and onto the ground just outside the passenger door. Leave a large rock conspicuously on the front seat. He

thinks someone broke into his vehicle and calls the police. With any luck, the cops will make a closer observation and realize that his passenger window is merely rolled down and that this is a false report. Everybody gets a laugh at his expense.

IT WORKS You're idling at a red light when your Target pulls up alongside. You rev your engine and give him the look. He takes the challenge and revs his motor. What he doesn't know is that this particular intersection is a "Fishing Hole" for motorcycle cops. You keep revving your engine so your Target stays focused on the traffic light. When the light turns green, you fake a fast start but then stay within the speed limit. He'll think he won

KNOW THE LINGO

FISHING HOLE
A particular stretch of road that police officers are known to position their speed traps.

until he sees red lights in his rearview mirror. And, as the cops plainly saw, you didn't exceed the speed limit. No harm, no ticket for you.

SHADES OF CHEECH AND CHONG Find a white powder with a slight shine to it, such as a cleaning agent. Pour one ounce into a plastic baggie. No fingerprints please, unless they belong to the Target. While someone buys lots of drinks for your Target, you place the bag barely under the driver's seat of the Target's vehicle. Then before he drives away from the bar, drop a dime to the local uniforms about this drunk driver. After stopping him, the cops will conduct a search of his vehicle. He gets a ride in the back seat of a squad car, while his own vehicle gets towed. Of course, it's not really a controlled substance in the baggie, but the police will be excited for a while.

SCENARIO

SOMEONE CUT YOU OFF IN TRAFFIC? TAKE IT EASY. TAIL HIM AND TEACH HIM A LESSON WHERE NO ONE ELSE CAN BE HURT—HIS OWN DRIVEWAY. . . .

OUT, DAMN SPOT On the underside of your vehicle's frame, attach a rectangular metal container supported on one end by means of a hinge and on the other end by a pin. Attach a wire to the opposite end of the pin and run this wire underneath the floorboard, through a hole and up by the driver's seat where it is easily accessible. Fill the metal container with old engine oil and lock the container in place with the pin. Drive to your Target's house, turn into his nice clean driveway, and pull on your end of the wire. The pin comes loose, one end of the metal container declines, and your Target has an oil spill on his driveway. To anyone watching, it merely looks like a car turning around in someone's drive.

IT HISSED AT ME I'm not talking about ordinary cockroaches, but rather the two- to three-inch-long Madagascar cockroaches, which hiss when they get disturbed. Imagine a couple dozen of these creepy critters running loose inside your Target's car. Of course, you left some edible goodies

under the driver's seat to keep them from creeping out right away. Just as your Target is motoring down the road, these little monsters start coming out, hissing at him and crawling all over him. That will be the fastest he ever gets out of a car.

SIR, ABOUT YOUR DOG ... You need something grim and drastic? Okay, obtain an old dog leash and patrol the highways until you find a fresh road kill. Scoop the carcass onto a plastic bag, put the dog collar around the neck of the deceased, and take him to your Target's vehicle. Attach the handle end of the leash to the rear bumper. Conceal the carcass underneath the vehicle so the driver won't notice it. While your Target is driving down the road, either the police or an outraged citizen will stop him. At least in the movie Chevy Chase had a script to work from, but what's this guy going to say? He didn't know he even had a dog, much less that it was dragging behind his pickup.

LOCATION 3

THE
GYM

The gym is the place you go to get in shape, socialize with friends, play a little sports, break a sweat, and maybe work off some steam. A good workout helps your mind cope with bad conditions at work, a demanding boss, or even the fact that life can sometimes have those moments that really suck. You may be engaging in some healthy mind and body exercise, but the guy lifting weights beside you or playing on the opposing sports team might not be coping as well as you are. His bad attitude could explode into verbal and physical violence against whoever he thinks is in his way. That someone could be you. Be ready for any confrontation.

SCENARIO

A MEATHEAD GETS ANGRY WHEN YOU ACCIDENTALLY KNOCK OVER HIS MUSCLE MILK ON YOUR WAY TO THE TREADMILL. HE REACHES OUT THINKING YOU'LL BE AN EASY FINISH. TEACH HIM THAT MUSCLES DON'T MEAN EVERYTHING. . . .

THE FINGER LOCK Use your left hand to grab the two outside fingers of opponent's right hand with your palm on top of the back of these two fingers. Follow this immediately by grasping his index and middle fingers in your right hand with your palm against the palm side of these two fingers. Pull down with your left hand and push back with your right hand. The backward pressure on his index and middle fingers can be used to force him to his knees. Is

there something you'd like to say to him at this point? You have his full attention. When practicing this move on your friends, be sure to ease the pressure before breaking any fingers. You really ought to keep your friends safe, happy, and impressed with what you can do if necessary.

THE AIKIDO WRIST TWIST Quickly reach out with both of your hands and grab his leading hand. With your fingertips in his palm and your thumbs on the back of his hand, twist his palm inward toward his chest with his thumb pointing out to the side away from his body. His wrist should now be bent toward his chest, which puts pressure on his wrist, elbow, and shoulder joints. His only way to relieve the

pressure is to go down on his knee or flip over sideways. Practice this one carefully so as not to cause muscle or joint damage. Have an understanding with him while he's down, and if necessary your knee is already positioned close to his face.

OR TRY THIS! Of course, you can always reverse the twist gambit by grabbing your opponent's right wrist with both of yours, then quickly stepping to his right side and turning so both of you are facing the same direction. Now, while holding his hand with your right hand, you raise his right arm and slide your left arm between his arm and his body. With your left hand make him bend his elbow upward. Place your left hand over your right hand and bend his wrist sharply downward. By keeping the back of his upper arm against your left elbow, his right elbow close to your left side, and his wrist held high but bent down, you can hold him easily. At this point, he may feel the need to drop to his knees, but he will gladly negotiate to your terms.

ARM LOCK Arm Locks are more difficult to do in a standing position, yet they can still be managed. With your right hand, thumb turned down, reach over and grab your opponent's right hand. Your thumb is on the back of his hand and your fingers are in his palm. Raise his hand to chest level and grab his wrist between the thumb and forefingers of your left hand, with your palm facing toward him. Move your left foot in front of his left foot while rotating your right foot clockwise until your body is perpendicular to his. Simultaneously rotate his right wrist and arm clockwise. Now slide your left

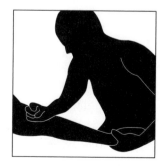

elbow on top of his right elbow and press down while bending your left knee slightly and rotating your upper body to your right. Lowering your left shoulder places more pressure on his locked-up elbow. Now, hold, throw, or punish.

GO ON THE DEFENSIVE: Breaking a Single-Wrist Hold

Some muscle-bound jerk got you first, grabbing your left wrist. What do you do? You immediately ball your left hand into a fist, then grab your fist with your right hand. In a spinning motion of your body and keeping your arms stiff at waist level, pull directly away from the opening between his thumb and his index finger.

That opening is the weak spot in his grip. Now, merely step away from him and go about your business. It makes him look weak. If his grip is strong enough to hold you, then soften him up with a fingertip jab to the throat or a hard kick to the shins, then spin away from his grasp.

GO ON THE DEFENSIVE: Breaking a Double-Wrist Hold

Since your attacker may use a different variation of the Wrist Hold, grabbing both your wrists at the same time, you need to know how to break this double hold. So, you take one step backward while moving your wrists toward each other. His mind will instinctively tell his arm and hand muscles to pull outward in order to oppose your inward wrist movement. Your muscles then use his outward movement to spread your wrists further apart while pulling him off balance toward you. This would be a good time to Snap Kick where he believes his manhood is located.

THIS GUY THINKS YOUR TIME'S UP WITH THE CHEST PRESS—EVEN THOUGH YOU'RE IN THE MIDDLE OF YOUR FIRST REP. NOW HE'S ALL HANDS, TRYING TO PULL YOU OFF THE MACHINE. . . .

PALM HEEL STRIKE Curl your fingers up to the top of your palm and rotate your hand backward until your palm faces outward and is perpendicular to your forearm. Then, bring that flat palm straight up from your waist with all your strength and into the base of his nose. It will bring tears to his eyes and blood to his nostrils. Don't wait around for him to recover.

JUJITSU SIDE HIP THROW Grab the back of your opponent's right elbow with your left hand while stepping forward with your left foot with the toes pointed out to the left. Spin to your left with your left foot planted until the back of your right hip blocks the front of his right hip. At the same time, move your right foot to the outside of his right leg while your right arm slides around his back at the waist. Hold tight and thrust your hips backward while bending forward at the waist to get him off balance. Simultaneously pull down and around on his right elbow and sweep your right thigh against his right thigh. He'll go flying.

FISH HOOKING There's a technique that is banned in sports martial arts and in competition during tournaments, but it is sometimes taught in self-defense classes. It's called Fish Hooking, and it's banned because of the risk of facial disfigurement to your opponent. But, when your life or own disfigurement is at risk, then you do what you have to in order to survive. It's just like a fishing hook buried in the mouth of a fish.

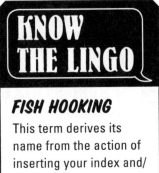

KNOW THE LINGO

FISH HOOKING

This term derives its name from the action of inserting your index and/ or middle finger(s) into your opponent's mouth or nostrils, digging in your fingernail(s), and jerking sideways.

WARNING! Keep your fingers hooked into his cheek and out of range of his teeth so your fingers don't get bit, and don't practice on your friends if you like their current facial appearance.

GO ON THE DEFENSIVE: Breaking a Rear Bear Hug

If someone grabs you in a Bear Hug from the rear with his arms over your arms, it usually means he's holding you for someone else to wreak havoc on your body. Since you, like most of us, are adverse to experiencing pain, you naturally want to get loose. Do this. Simultaneously, step sideways to your left while dropping your weight until your knees are flexed and raising your elbows outward and up. You've loosened his hold, plus he is now leaning forward slightly and off balance. Spin to your right and either drive your right elbow into his ribs or throw a short left-hand punch to his face. If he has grabbed you too low around the arms and body for this to work, then smash the heel of your shoe into his kneecap, or stomp on his instep first.

However, if your attacker grabs you in a Bear Hug from the rear and his arms are underneath your arms, then a different method is used to break the hold. Step sideways to the right with your right foot, then drop your weight slightly to make his upper body lean forward while you bend over and grab the back of his right ankle with both hands. Immediately pull up on his right ankle while blocking the upper part of his right leg with your butt. The pressure this move puts on his right knee, which is built to only bend in one direction, will cause him to fall backward. Be aware though: If your attacker tries to hold tight to your body when you bend over, slam your hips back against his stomach first in order to loosen his grip.

FIGHTING STYLE

No-holds barred: When you're out-matched, out fought, and desperate to survive the physical altercation, that's when anything goes. Forget about the Queensberry Rules of fighting for gentle-man. Forget about any concept of the old American perception of fighting fair. You are about to have your teeth handed to you afterward in a sandwich baggy by some bully out to make a reputation for being bad. You're risking broken bones and potential disfigurement. All's fair now.

SCENARIO

YOU JUST FINISHED ALL YOUR REPS ON THE BENCH PRESS, AND NOW YOU'VE GOT ONE OF THOSE SMALL GYM TOWELS IN HAND TO WIPE IT DOWN. INSTEAD THIS JUICING FREAK COMES UP AND—GRABBING YOU BY THE SHIRT—LOOKS LIKE HE'S ABOUT TO WIPE THE MACHINE WITH YOU. . . .

USING YOUR HEAD You bend over slightly like you're about to put the towel away, then throw the towel in his face. While he's distracted, lower your head and butt hard into his solar plexus. You now have two choices. One, quickly grab the backs of his ankles or the front of his pant's cuffs and pull up while you're still bent over, or two, snap the back of your head up into the point of his chin. Lights out.

KNOW THE LINGO

SOLAR PLEXUS
A dense collection of nerves in the abdomen behind one's stomach.

PLEASE DON'T GRAB MY LAPELS For some reason, when guys want to act tough and don't think they'll have any problem with the person they're picking on, they like to grab their victim by the lapels or shirtfront. If it happens to you, place your hands together in the praying position with the fingertips pointed up. You can say a short prayer if you're so inclined, but keep it down to a couple of words, because you want to immediately drive your hands upward between his wrists with your elbows spread. His hands will be forced away from your lapels. Now grab his sleeves or forearms while you step back and pull him forward off balance. Yep, it's time for a groin kick again. You saw it coming, but he didn't.

PARDON MY FOOT Another variation to use on the guy who grabs your lapels is the Stomach Throw. Of course, this is assuming you have no obstacles behind you. When the tough guy grabs your lapels and pushes you backward, you grab the outside of his sleeves or elbows. Use his pushing motion to pull the top part of his body off balance and toward you. Drop your weight in a backward rolling motion so the two of you form a hoop shape. Curl your right leg up, knee to your chest, with your foot in his stomach. Continue rolling the hoop while you kick your right leg upward. Hold tightly to his sleeves. He will fly over your head and land flat on his back. Flip over to your stomach and give him a chop to the throat.

IF YOU HAVE THE LUXURY OF PLANNING ON HOW TO GET BACK AT SOME LOCKER-ROOM KNUCKLEHEAD, TRY CONNING HIM INTO A KARATE CLASS AT YOUR GYM. LITTLE DOES HE KNOW . . . .

KARATE MISHAPS During the instruction, be sure to deliver some obviously uncontrolled kicks and punches to your Target—not enough to stop the class, just enough to enjoy hitting him. Of course, you apologize for your beginner's lack of control and you duck your head in humility, keeping him from seeing that huge grin on your face because you just got in some free shots.

YOU'RE NOT DOING THIS RIGHT Let's say you do have karate experience, so you offer to teach him at a gym or some other public place. Carefully show him how to block a punch or a kick. Do it in slow motion so he understands. Then punch him. Apologize for hitting him, but explain that he needs to block correctly to effectively counter your action. Demonstrate the blocking movement in slow motion again. Ask if he's ready. Then punch him hard. Repeat the apology. Eventually, you give up in obvious disgust because he just isn't learning. Offer to start instruction again at a later time when he's ready to learn. How long can you continue this scenario? Depends on how gullible he is.

WHAT'D YOU SIT IN? Forget getting physical. After he's changed into the proper karate garb, stick around the locker room and get a hold of your Target's dress slacks. Withdraw a nice glob of petroleum jelly from its container and carefully deposit this mass in one of the rear pockets of his dress slacks. The trick here is figuring how much petroleum jelly you can use without the Target detecting it when he puts his pants on. It works best if the glob is more flat like a piece of flexible cardboard as opposed to round like a marble. The longer he sits, the more the jelly penetrates the cloth until he has a shiny gross spot on the seat of his pants.

FIGHTING STYLE

Karate: It teaches some of the best basic moves in martial arts for both offense and defense. I prefer the tae kwon do style brought over from Korea, but you will also find styles from Japan and China being taught in the United States as well. Most are good choices; however, if you choose your local martial arts school merely because you like its flashy movie title name, you may be following a teacher who has broken away from internationally recognized organizations and you may or may not be getting your money's worth. Check out your intended teacher's credentials, not just his website, before you sign that contract. Also inquire if you are allowed to participate in at least one free session in order to ensure this is what you want to do.

GO ON THE DEFENSIVE: Breaking a Front Stranglehold

Let's say your Target does know a thing or two and puts you in a Front Stranglehold. Here's what to do *quickly*—because one, you don't want him to push you against a wall where you have no movement, and two, lack of oxygen to the brain is bad. Put your palms together at your waist with fingertips pointed up like you're about to pray. Jam both hands upward between his arms at the inside of his elbows, the weak spot in his stranglehold. The impact of your rising arms at the inside of his elbow joints causes his stranglehold to break away to each side. While you're standing that close to your opponent it is good time for a Front Snap Kick to the body part of your choice. It's a free shot.

GO ON THE DEFENSIVE: Breaking a Rear Stranglehold

Your attacker came up behind you when you weren't expecting it and wrapped his forearm across your windpipe. The blood supply to your brain is rapidly diminishing. Time is important if you don't want to pass out from lack of oxygen. Quickly raise one knee as high as you can and kick backward so your heel hits his kneecap. If you're wearing a solid shoe, don't worry about that cracking noise—your footgear is okay. Now, turn around and disable him if he's still standing.

WARNING! Since kneecaps tend to be fragile, do not practice this on your friends if you wish to keep them.

Another method to break a Rear Stranglehold is to draw your left arm forward, make a fist, and then drive your left elbow into the attacker's solar plexus or ribs. He'll open up like a door. If your attacker holds you so tightly that there is not much room to deliver an elbow strike with much force, nod your head forward and suddenly drive it back into his nose or chin. This hard, abrupt contact will bring tears to his eyes and jar him loose enough for you to drive that elbow into your Target. Step away.

Just in case you want another option to loosen up your attacker's Rear Stranglehold, here's the Instep Stomp. No doubt you've seen it used a couple of times by grappling opponents during ultimate cage-fighting matches. It seems the foot's instep can be a fragile set of bones, especially if the striker is wearing shoes with hard heels. To use this movement, raise your striking foot as high as you can, then drive it directly down on the top of your opponent's arch so that the edge of your heel has all the power you can muster. He won't be able to pursue you any faster than he can painfully limp.

SCENARIO

THERE'S THIS REAL JERK WHO ALWAYS SEEMS TO GET THE GYM AT THE SAME TIME AS YOU, AND ALWAYS FINDS A PLACE RIGHT NEXT TO YOU TO CHANGE, AND ALWAYS RIDES YOU ABOUT HOW HE CAN LIFT MORE WEIGHTS, PLAY BETTER BASKETBALL, AND RUN FARTHER THAN YOU. HE'S OBNOXIOUS, BUT NOT WORTH GETTING INTO A FIGHT WITH, SO WHAT ARE YOU GOING TO DO? HAVE YOU THOUGHT ABOUT THE ART OF EMBARRASSMENT?. . .

THE EMPEROR HAS NO CLOTHES Watch what model of lock he uses on his gym locker, then buy one just like it. If his is an old one, you may have to rough up your new purchase, or rub its surface so it appears dull in the same places. Observe over his shoulder until you get his combination. The next time he gets ready to head for the showers with just his towel, surreptitiously swap locks. Then take his towel off the hook outside the shower room. Now he can't open his locker and he has nothing to cover up his nakedness.

PEBBLE IN THE SHOE Find a rock to put in his favorite running shoes—not one of those smooth pebbles from a river bottom, but rather a small rock with a sharp angle, sometimes found in decorative lawn gravel. The next time you get access to the Target's shoes at the gym, lift up the inner sole, place the pointed rock underneath where his heel will come down, and glue the rock in place. Replace the inner sole to its usual position. With the right-sized rock, neither so big that it gets noticed right away, nor so small as to be ineffective, your Target will acquire a sore heel and wonder why.

STUCK ON YOU Fill a couple of small balloons with super-glue and then fold over the end. Or, you can make your glue time bombs out of small squares of folded cellophane. Now, get your hands on your Target's sneakers. Place the glue bombs carefully into the toe of your Target's shoes. When he inserts his foot, his toes will squish out the glue and stick to everything, including each other. If you've ever tried to separate things that have been superglued together, you know what fun this is.

SCENARIO

SOME MEN NEVER GROW UP; THEY STILL HAVE THAT HIGH-SCHOOL LOCKER-ROOM MENTALITY AT THE GYM. IF SOME GUY'S GIVING YOU GRIEF IN THE SHOWER, SHOW HIM WHO THE BETTER MAN IS. . . .

THAT'S A NEW LOOK YOU HAVE THERE Mix stay-fast or permanent dye in his personal shampoo bottle. Yellow is probably best because many shampoos are yellow or gold in color and therefore the new addition won't be as noticeable until it is way too late for him, but whatever you do, match the color of the dye to the color of his shampoo. Now, picture him with bright yellow hair, or whatever color he ended up with. That and a suit make a real fashion statement in a conservative business meeting. And if he works construction with a bunch of macho guys, you can imagine their reaction to his new hair color.

OR TRY THIS! If your Target uses some color of shampoo other than yellow, here's an alternative. Get a liquid hair removal product from your local discount store. Read the instructions carefully to see what quantity is needed to do the job. Because you are diluting the hair remover liquid with shampoo, the resulting combination won't be as powerful, but that's okay. If his hair gradually falls out, he may think it's due to a genetic condition and keep on using your devilish concoction. By the time he finishes the shampoo bottle, he will resemble a naked mole rat. Make sure the product you choose has no warnings about damage to the eyes.

THE HEAD SCRATCHER Head lice are parasitic wingless insects that live on people's heads and feed on their blood. The adult louse is about the size of a sesame seed, while their eggs are like a flake of dandruff. Since children in the age range of three to eleven get head lice most often, and lice are so contagious, other family members also get the little buggers. The victim feels the itch and then scratches the infected area, which results in sores. You could easily insert captured head lice onto your Target's towel hanging in a gym locker or hanging on a hook outside the shower room. He'll be scratching his head wondering where they came from.

WARNING! Be sure to protect yourself and your clothing from infestation during this clandestine mission.

IT ITCHES At one of those stores that sells oddball gags, buy some packages of itching powder. Spread this powder in your Target's gym bag while he's busy being an ass in the shower. If you sprinkle the powder inside his socks, be sure to replace the socks exactly as you found them so he doesn't suspect they've been tampered with. To increase the confusion as to source of the problem, apply powder to only one sock in the pair. If you sprinkle powder inside his T-shirt, apply it to the backside of the shirt so he'll have a hard time scratching that itch. With a back itch, most guys rub against an open door frame to relieve that spot they can't quite reach. He'll look like a bear rubbing on a tree. Now there's a sophisticated sight for your memory page.

OR TRY THIS! Can't find itching powder? No problem. During the summer, take a weed or botany guidebook along for a hike in the woods. Look at the pictures and compare them to the weeds in front of you. Poison ivy grows wild and is free to all. Collect several leaves, but stuff your specimens into an airtight bag. Wear gloves and don't let the leaves touch your clothes or shoes. The plant's oil causes a

rash on human skin, and once the oil is on a person's clothes it can be transferred to his skin by simple contact, so generously brush the collected leaves against your Target's clean underwear in his locker or gym bag. He won't be able to keep his hands off himself.

SCENARIO

SICK OF THAT GUY STRUTTING AROUND THE CLUB WITH HIS RACQUET OVER HIS SHOULDER TELLING EVERYONE HOW UNDEFEATABLE HE IS? TIME TO TAKE HIM DOWN A FEW NOTCHES. . . .

DIDN'T SEE YOU For those times when your opponent is close to violence and is making your life miserable one way or another, you need to get more devious. One way to get even with your tormentor is to have what looks like a plausible accident. For instance, he plays racquetball at the local Y. Doesn't make any difference if he's as good as he claims. In any case, you challenge him. He hits the ball, and now it's your turn. Here, timing is everything. As you swing at the ball, your follow-through manages to somehow catch him in the head. Head wounds bleed buckets even with slight damage. You apologize profusely and offer to pay for the stitches. He'll wonder later if it really was an accident, but you're not telling.

THAT'S GONNA COST HIM The place I play racquetball has a glass wall through which observers can watch the game, plus three wooden walls. The door into the court is also made of glass, and since it swings on hinges there is a small amount of play in the door when it closes. This amount of play means that the door, if hit right, can be broken. My gym goes through about two doors a year at several thousand dollars a door. So aim your shots to drive your Target backwards toward the glass door, especially when he's already tired. One awkward body slam by him into the door may make it shatter. Hint: this works best on amateurs. Pros will wait for the ball to come off the back wall.

THE KISS OF DEATH Chances are you've seen this guy in the locker room in his underwear. Buy some underwear in the same brand and size as your Target. Wash the underwear several times so it doesn't look new. After all, you want his significant other to believe this is actually his piece of clothing. Put a lipstick kiss on the front just above the flap opening, and in large letters write a short note. The note should say something like "Call me when you get home."

Place this in his gym bag. (You know a guy like this has his wife do his laundry.) The lipstick gives the appearance he had a fun time with someone else and didn't realize that other female had written a note on his clothing.

THE
GAME

Sports are supposed to be tough, whether they're mental or physical excursions. Therefore there are plenty of opportunities for things to erupt and get out of hand. This could provide you with some tricky situations where you'll need to fight your way out. But it could also provide some opportunities to take a swing at your Target.

SCENARIO

YOU MADE IT TO THE POOL TABLE BEFORE TROUBLE STARTED. IT'S A FRIENDLY GAME, BUT SOMEBODY TAKES OFFENSE. SURE, IT COULD BE A RIGHTEOUS BEEF, BUT THAT'S NOT THE POINT. HE'S GETTING PHYSICAL. YOU'D RATHER HAVE ANOTHER BEER AND GET NEXT TO THAT CUTE BLOND OVER BY THE WALL. BUT, OH WELL. . . .

POOL SHARK'S CHOICE A pool cue is thick and heavy at one end, thin and light at the other, and subject to breaking in the middle if you swing it like a bat. You've got one shot at him, so make it a good one. A better use is to pull the stick back to your side and then lunge forward with it, using it like a spear aimed at the belly or face of your attacking opponent. Then whack him.

EIGHT BALL IN THE SIDE POCKET See those round colorful things rolling around the table? Pick up the nearest one. This gives you two choices. If you have no room to maneuver, then you'll probably have to swing your hand holding the pool ball like a weighted club. But if you've got room, then wind up and throw your best fastball pitch and grab a second ball in case he ducked. It works in the movies, but you'd better have some accuracy.

A SCRATCH IN TIME Get the tip of your cue too far under the cue ball and shoot it across the table at this shark. Be warned though: you better have good aim as you only have one shot before he comes across the table looking for blood.

HOOPS AND HOOPLA Today's game of basketball has bigger and stronger players than ever, plus they get more physical to intimidate the opposition and muscle the ball away. (Must be a carryover from the Vietnam era when we played "Jungle rules" in the base camps.) In any case, the game changed, and a lot more elbows get thrown if the refs don't keep an eagle eye. In the mass confusion under the basket, you have the option of tripping, hitting, and/or throwing a hard elbow. Make sure it's a mob scene, not one-on-one, so you have a better chance of getting away with your "foul." And wait until the ref has his back turned. Oops, must be a foul there somewhere since there was an injury, but who knows who inflicted it? Sorry.

I THOUGHT YOU WERE WATCHING This one's for if you have to play on the same team as your Target. You've got the ball in the other team's court and you're passing the ball around waiting for one of your men to get open enough to take a good shot. Your Target moves quickly to get away from the man guarding him, and just before he's about to turn around, you throw the ball hard at his head. Damn, he should have been more aware of what's going on in the court if he wants the team to win. Obviously his fault.

OH CRAP He likes to talk crap. Might as well smell like it. Grab a plastic bag and a stick and go for a walk through the neighborhood to collect whatever the dogs have deposited in the grass. Now gain access to his basketball sneakers so you can fill in those treads with dog doo. Spray a coat of epoxy on the soles to enclose the bad odor. After he plays on them for a while, the spray will wear off and the stink will begin.

SOME ADVICE . . .

If you're involved in any sport where mass confusion ensues and your Target is in the middle of it, jump in. Naturally, you're looking to get in some free shots, but you're too late. Somebody else has already dusted his noggin for him and he's not seeing straight. He doesn't know that though. Play a psychological game; quietly let him know that you were the one who dumped his ass in the dirt, and the next chance you get, you're going to do it twice as hard. He doesn't know you're taking credit for what someone else did, but as long as he went down hard enough, in the back of his mind he will start to fear you. Just don't push your luck too far.

EVERYONE TAKES PART IN YOUR BEER LEAGUE TO HAVE FUN—EXCEPT THIS GUY. HE GETS BENT OUT OF SHAPE OVER EVERY PLAY THAT'S MADE (EVEN THOUGH HE'S ACTUALLY THE WORST ONE ON THE TEAM). NOW HE'S STARTING TO RUIN YOUR FUN. . . .

LOOKS LIKE HE'S OUT The local softball league is a little more difficult to work with and avoid obvious detection, but hey, as the bikers say in Sturgis, "crap occurs." At least that's what the polite ones say. So, it's a nice sunny day, the beer's flowing, and everybody's having a great day at the ball diamond. Then it happens. Maybe a throw to stop a runner headed for second base is badly aimed? Of course, sliding into base sometimes makes awkward contact, doesn't it? You see where I'm going here, but they're all accidents, aren't they? Apologies are easy; pain takes a while to go away.

PITCHER, PITCHER If you have the opportunity to pitch against this guy, it's your lucky day. A good bean ball has always been used to set a guy straight in the majors. Why not bring the practice to your beer league? Don't be too obvious by aiming for his head or by actually positioning yourself as if you're throwing at him. Just cut the pitch inside. No one will be the wiser—except you.

HOME RUNS WITH ALUMINUM Chances are this knucklehead is the kind of guy who stands outside the cage "cheering" on his teammates as they bat. Sure, he's been told plenty of times about the danger, but he waves it off. Lucky for you. Next time you're up to bat and knock one out, accidentally let go of the bat and let it fly in his direction. The loud, hollow *thunk* the bat makes when it connects with his groin will sound sweeter than when you connected with the pitch.

THIS GLORY DAYS A-HOLE DOESN'T SHUT UP ABOUT HOW GOOD HIS TEAM WAS WAY BACK WHEN THEY WON STATE. LET HIS BIG MOUTH AND BIGGER EGO BE HIS DOWNFALL. . . .

HOME GAME If your Target is dumb enough to let you play a friendly game of touch football on his lawn, you're halfway there. If he's not amiable to using his lawn as home field, then you'll have to arrange for an impromptu session that strays onto his turf, or else have the friendly competition when he's not home. This game should be played in late fall after his sprinkler system is shut down for the winter. As you play, carefully note where all the sprinkler heads are and step heavily on most of them without being obvious. He won't know he has a leakage problem until the system is turned on next spring.

TAKE YOUR FREE SHOTS At this point, it doesn't make any difference if you join his team or the opposing team; however, you will probably draw less suspicion if you're both on the same team. It gives you plausible deniability. Sooner or later there will be a dog pile on the player with the ball. Choosing carefully so that your Target is part of the dog pile, you jump in with lots of enthusiasm and several clandestine elbows, knees, and punches. Hey, everybody takes his chances in a football game.

GO LONG! Ever been hit in the face with a football on a cold day? It hurts—a lot. When your Target is on your team, offer to play quarterback. Set a pattern that has your Target cut across the field in front of you before turning up to catch a pass down the sideline. He'll be so intent on his route, he'll never see it coming. When he cuts across the middle to get to the sideline, launch the ball right at his head. Say you were trying to connect with the guy running the middle route.

SCENARIO

SOCCER PLAYERS ARE SOME OF THE BIGGEST EGOMANIACS YOU'LL COME ACROSS. CHANCES ARE IF YOU'RE PLAYING IN A LEAGUE, THERE ARE PLENTY OF PEOPLE WHOSE ASS YOU WANT TO KICK. CHOOSE THE WORST OF THE BUNCH, AND GO AFTER HIM. . . .

FÚTBOL In Spanish speaking countries, the game of soccer is known as fútbol. Which works because the game is played mainly with the feet. There are collisions between players, and the opposing side is often tripped, by accident of course, especially if the referee is looking the other direction. Since it's hard to criticize enthusiasm during a play, you can probably get by with a lot during an amateur game. And, once again, if you're on the same side, you obviously have no motive for disabling your own teammate. Look aggrieved by your Target's injuries.

WHY'S EVERYBODY STARING AT ME? Want to put your opponent off his game? Get a large and imposing friend to show up at the field whenever your Target has practice or a game. Have the friend stare at your Target while he plays. Sooner or later, he will feel the glare and turn to see what's going on. Be sure your friend is imposing enough that the Target won't go over to ask why the hulk is staring at him. Once seen, have your friend disappear until the next game. Your Target will start worrying who's after him and what he is going to do.

THE GAME OF LOVE Your tormentor has given you a lot of grief and you want to get him back. A guy with this big of an ego has some serious insecurities. Figure out which of the women in the stands is his girlfriend or wife. While you're playing, look to her in the stands and smile, maybe even give a wave. Make sure he notices. Chat her up after the match and figure out what Beckham-like qualities her man is missing. Whatever she wants and he lacks in their relationship suddenly becomes your strong points. Redefine yourself as the best thing since Don Juan discovered he had a way with women. Once you seduce her, tell him. The bigger the ego, the bigger the fall.

SCENARIO

THIS JERKWAD COMES INTO THE NINETEENTH HOLE RUNNING HIS MOUTH ABOUT HOW AWESOME HIS HANDICAP IS AND HOW MANY BIRDIES HE SHOT HIS LAST ROUND. ACCORDING TO HIM, EVERYONE ELSE IS A LOSER. SOMEONE NEEDS TO SHUT HIM UP AND THAT SOMEONE IS YOU. . . .

WAS THAT A HOOK OR A SLICE? Spend some time on the driving range with your Target. Only in this case, instead of seeing how far you can drive a golf ball, you practice your hooks and slices because you don't know which side of you he will be standing on. About the third tee of actual play, talk him into standing slightly forward and to one side so he can offer helpful suggestions on your swing. Then, hook or slice badly as is appropriate. Not your fault—golfing accidents are like acts of God, they just happen.

WARNING! Keep the ball low to avoid concussions and permanent injuries.

PLAYING BENT For the Target who loves golf, alter his playing equipment to increase his frustration with the game. Select only some of his golf clubs and very carefully bend the shaft of each selected club in a slightly different direction so the club face doesn't strike the ball at the angle it's supposed to hit. Leave some of the clubs as they are, which allows him to think he's still got the proper swing when he uses that set of clubs. The clubs with altered shafts will drive him wild because his swing will seldom produce the results he desires. And, a bad day at golf usually carries over to the rest of the player's outlook on daily life. Have a nice day.

TICK, TICK, TICK Here's a real bloodsucker. In July 2008, a United flight was delayed because a passenger found ticks crawling around in economy class. Now imagine a couple dozen ticks crawling around on your Target. They make no noise, give no warning, and the victim doesn't know the tick is there until he feels a lump on his skin. These guys are the ninjas of the insect world. To collect them, wear white clothes (makes ticks easily seen) and walk through some tall grass or a wooded area that deer frequent. Place your catch in a small, ventilated container. The next time he plays golf, empty your container inside his golf bag. They'll find him later.

WARNING! Some ticks carry Lyme disease or Rocky Mountain spotted fever.

SCENARIO

YOU LIKE HANGING OUT AT THE LOCAL BOWLING ALLEY AND HAVING A FEW FRIENDLY GAMES, BUT LATELY THERE'S BEEN THAT ONE OBNOXIOUS GUY WHO'S BEEN TAKING ALL THE FUN OUT IT. HE JUST KEEPS ON HASSLING YOU, MAKES FUN OF YOUR BOWLING STYLE, LAUGHS AT YOUR SCORE, AND MAKES IT A MISSION TO POINT OUT ANY MISTAKE YOU MAKE. GOD FORBID YOU SHOULD END UP WITH A 7-10 SPLIT. . . .

FOUL Watch to see what resin bag he uses to help his grip on the ball. Either buy one like it and empty the resin contents or make a bag exactly like his. Fill your bag with unscented baby powder and switch your bag with his. He'll have little control over his next thrown ball when it slips out before he's ready. It's a whole new game.

SLIPPERY SOLES Soles of bowling shoes are supposed to slide gracefully across the floor when the bowler steps forward and releases his ball down the alley. But what happens when one shoe gets a tacky substance on the bottom? That's when his foot comes to a speed bump stop and a quick hop trying to keep his balance. He'll be lucky to keep the ball in his own alley. How to do it? Before the game, you pour a little of your favorite brown cola on a rag and smear it on the shoe sole of whichever of his feet is forward when he releases the ball. It's trickier to accomplish this task while the game is in progress, but it can still be done. Wait until he's keeping score, then place the wet rag flat on the ground where he will step on it without noticing. Quickly dispose of rag.

BUTTER FINGERS Get a game going against this guy and use it as an opportunity to bowl him over, literally. Since he's such a chump, he'll probably be standing chatting to everyone around when your up bowling your sets. Position yourself carefully so that when you extend your arm back and accidentally let your fingers slip out of the ball it connects with him. Oops.

WARNING! Do not release the ball too high or else there is the chance it will hit him in the head.

There Was This One Time . . .

I used to go to the dog track with an old man, and just for fun, as he suggested, we'd bet between us as to who would have the most winning tickets by the end of the night. Didn't make any difference whether you had a Win, Place, or Show ticket, if your ticket paid off at the window, that ticket counted as one win on the side bet. And, I'll be damned, at the end of almost every race, he reached into his pocket and pulled out a ticket that won. He kicked my ass regularly on our side bet. It took me a while to realize his winning ticket didn't always come from the same pocket. He'd purchase several different tickets, then memorize which dog was on which ticket and which pocket he'd put that ticket in. He only pulled out his winning tickets to collect from me.

LOCATION 5

SOCIAL
FUNCTIONS

Other than your spouse, you don't get to pick who your family members are, but you're usually stuck with these characters through the good and the bad. Same goes with friends, acquaintances, and associates (though I guess you *did* get to pick them). You don't have to love everything they do, but you do have to put up with their idiosyncrasies and annoying habits . . . or do you?

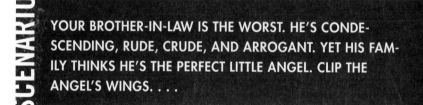

SCENARIO

YOUR BROTHER-IN-LAW IS THE WORST. HE'S CONDESCENDING, RUDE, CRUDE, AND ARROGANT. YET HIS FAMILY THINKS HE'S THE PERFECT LITTLE ANGEL. CLIP THE ANGEL'S WINGS. . . .

SORRY, MA Does your Target enjoy the occasional viewing of a risqué video? If so, help him add to his collection until it becomes too large to successfully conceal in a small area. Every time you stop by his place, leave a porno or two behind. When the collection is large enough, that's when you, using a fake name, invite his mother to a surprise party for him at his house. Make sure it's a night you're there, and queue up a video to play right when Mom arrives. She'll never let him forget. And, you don't have to buy videos, just loan him some borrowed from others.

THE SCARLET GIFT CARD For a different twist on the surprise video party, buy your Target a birthday gift card for the local adult bookstore. Tell him the card is only good for a limited time. After all, you don't want to be following him around for days. Then, when he does go to the adult store, you're waiting outside to film him going in and to show him coming out with a package in his hands. Be sure the name of the store is featured somewhere in the film. Copies should go to his preacher, his mom, his girlfriend and her friends. . . .

YEP, THAT'S DEFINITELY HIM Find an embarrassing photo of your Target. I'm not talking about that cute little photo when he was five and had no baby teeth in the bottom of his smile. No, I'm referring to the time he got smashed at a party and his "friends" dressed him up in pantyhose and bra, or get a copy of his mug shot when the cops busted him for something minor. Take your own photo opportunity if you have to. Blow the photo up to poster size and place it in his front yard on a morning when he's sleeping late. Then call his church, boss, and local newspaper. The neighbors will soon see the reason for all the drive-by activity.

YOU LIKE YOUR WIFE'S BEST FRIEND. YOU HATE HER HUS-
BAND. BUT IT DOESN'T LOOK LIKE SHE'LL BE LOSING THE
BALL-AND-CHAIN ANY TIME SOON. SO RATHER THAN
SKIP OUT ON THE INVITE-ONLY DINNER HE'S THROWING
TO SHOW OFF HIS HAUL FROM A WEEKLONG CARIBBEAN
FISHING TRIP, GO, AND HAVE SOME FUN. . . .

SMALL CLEANING PROBLEM After he cleans, filets, wraps, and places his catch in the freezer, it's time to take action. Bide your time until you have access to these packages of fish. Makes no difference whether you get to them shortly after they got wrapped or while they are in the freezer. Carefully unwrap the packages. Place a couple of worms between the filets and rewrap the fish so no one can tell the packages have been tampered with. He's the kind of guy who will make a show of unwrapping and showing off his catch. He'll have something to show off, for sure. Appetite over.

I LOST MY APPETITE Just about any deceased small animal close to ripe will serve your purpose. You don't want a great stench yet—that will come later. Conceal the animal's carcass inside the propane grill but out of immediate sight. Underneath the burners works fine. Make sure the animal is near enough to the flames so that when he lights the grill, the heat will bring out the stiff odor of something other than the tantalizing meat he intended to cook. Makes no difference how good the chef is—that other smell will override his culinary skills.

BURNT OFFERINGS Pack up your cordless drill and several different-sized metal drill bits. Raise the lid on his propane grill and remove the cooking grates. Determine the diameter of the holes in his burner. Drill out the holes of the burners on one side to a larger size. Don't make the holes so large that the flame scorches his eyebrows—just large enough that one end of the grill cooks food three times faster than the other end of the burner.

SCENARIO YOUR WIFE'S BEST FRIEND IS INSUFFERABLE. SHE'S CONSTANTLY CRITIQUING WHATEVER YOU'RE DRINKING AND NEVER BELIEVES IT'S UP TO SNUFF. WHEN SHE INVITES YOU TWO OVER FOR A WINE AND CHEESE PARTY, IT'S YOUR CHANCE TO SHOW HER WHAT WHINING IS REALLY ABOUT. . . .

THE WINE CONNOISSEUR: PART 1 If your Target has a small refrigeration unit known as a wine cooler where she stores her collection in order to keep it at a constant recommended temperature, all you have to do is unplug the unit from the wall. If pulling the plug would be visibly noticed, then flip the circuit breaker. By the time she notices the problem, her wine is no longer maintained at the proper temp. And, while room temperature may not actually affect the taste, she will have the perception that her wine is ruined.

THE WINE CONNOISSEUR: PART 2 If your Target displays her wine bottles on a wooden rack where the mouth of each bottle is slanted down to keep the cork swollen so it maintains a good seal, here's a different plan: Purchase a bottle of cheap red wine. Pour it into a plastic squirt bottle and allow the contents to sit in the open air for a few days. The next time you get close to her wine rack, squirt your cheap wine on the mouth end of some of her bottles. Allow the mess to drip on the floor, especially if the rack sits over a carpet. Wipe off the up side of the bottles, because any true dripping would appear on the lower side. She assumes her corks went bad and throws out the supposedly leaking bottles. Free wine for you.

THE WINE CONNOISSEUR: PART 3

Since most expensive wines are corked, you should acquire a large syringe with a long needle. Carefully pry up a small piece of the foil covering the top of the cork in the bottle of wine you have selected. Gently insert the needle between the cork and the glass mouth of the bottle. Tip the bottle and draw out the plunger on the syringe. Remove as much wine as possible, withdraw the needle, and squirt the purloined wine into your glass. Repeat as necessary. You now have the choice of letting her assume the almost-empty bottle is due to evaporation, or you can use the method in reverse to insert a cheap wine into her bottle.

OR TRY THIS! As an alternative to the above Way, after you remove enough of her wine for you to have an enjoyable glassful, you then inject vinegar into her wine bottle. After all, wine does eventually turn into vinegar if the container has an air leak. With a delicate repositioning of the foil over the cork, your Target won't notice that her wine has been tampered with, and after the bottle has already been opened by her, any disturbance in the foil becomes a moot point. Though, if you're present at the opening, you might want to employ a little distraction to be on the safe side.

SCENARIO

THE LAST TIME YOU HAD PEOPLE OVER FOR DINNER, YOUR FRIEND'S HUSBAND BASICALLY RAISED HIS FOODIE NOSE AT YOUR OFFERINGS. HE WAS VERY VOCAL ABOUT THE SELECTION BEING OFFERED AND HOW IT WASN'T UP TO THE STANDARDS OF HIS COOKING. WELL, NOW HE'S ABOUT TO SHOW OFF HIS COOKING SKILLS AT A DINNER PARTY AND YOU'RE ABOUT TO SHOW OFF YOUR REVENGE TACTICS. . . .

AIIEE, CHIHUAHUA Invest in a bottle of habanero pepper sauce and conceal it in your pocket. When you have the opportunity, open up the Target's silverware drawer. Carefully rub habanero sauce on the eating surfaces of all the knives, forks, and spoons, but skip the handles. Just a light film, nothing visible. Everything he eats after that will have a bite to it. On meats and such he may not be aware why he has a new flavoring to his foods, but it definitely explodes his taste buds when it comes time for desserts and ice cream. Wear latex gloves, and remember not to lick your fingers or rub your eyes.

THE HAIRY HOST The food smells great and has an excellent presentation. Looks like the evening will be a success, but wait, what's that? One of the guests sticks his fork into what is intended to be his next mouthful and there it is, a long hair embedded in the food. Of course, you've ensured that the hair in the food is the exact color and length as the hair on the host's head. It's safe to say the rest of the evening will be a little hairy as each guest thinks about the surprise in the host's cuisine.

THE OTHER PROTEIN In more primitive times, our ancestors ate whatever gave nourishment to their bodies. Sometimes they even ate bugs for the protein those little critters provided. However, in today's society it takes a hardy individual to consume a bug. Most people tend to sue if they find an insect in their restaurant meal. Of course, when your Target gives that sumptuous dinner party, you could place

half a bug sticking prominently out of the side or top of someone's food serving. It helps if the bug is obvious and a different color than the food. Make this serving the last onto the table and the other diners will wonder where the other half of the bug is.

SCENARIO

"OH! AREN'T THEY THE PERFECT COUPLE?" EVERYONE IN YOUR FAMILY FAWNS OVER YOUR PHILANDERING COUSIN AND HIS TOO-GOOD-FOR-HIM GIRLFRIEND. AND THE JERK RUBS IN THE FACT HOW HOT SHE IS AND HOW MUCH ASS HE'S GETTING ON THE SIDE WHENEVER YOU'RE IN PRIVATE. . . .

IF I WERE HIM Even if you don't seduce her, frequently mention little bullet points such as, "If I had a girlfriend as great as you, then I'd do . . . or buy you . . . "—whatever it takes to make her unhappy with how much he doesn't do for her. You can promise the moon because you'll never have to deliver. She's not your girlfriend. But, you will be able to sit back and enjoy the fights that soon follow as she comes to realize that he is an insensitive clod who isn't treating her right. Personal relationships are so hard to maintain.

HEAR THOSE BELLS? If your Target hasn't proposed to his girlfriend yet, you start showing her bridal magazines and telling her what a beautiful bride she'll make . . . some day. Insinuate that if he hasn't discussed marriage yet then he's probably got a little something on the side and doesn't want to get tied down to just one. Or, discretely relate a "biological clock is running" story about someone who married late in life even though everyone thought she would never get a man. It helps if you have an actual person to point to as the woman in the story. A little truth makes the lie more believable. The more she thinks about her own clock, she'll quickly make his free-and-easy bachelorhood uncomfortable.

FOR WHOM THE BELLS TOLL If your Target has proposed to his girlfriend, then you drop subtle hints that he has trouble committing to just one woman, especially if you have knowledge of him previously dating two girls at the same time at any point in his life, and you have a witness to confirm the story. A small fact goes a long way toward agitating the green-eyed monster who resides within most people. Current cell phone photos of him laughing with another female in a bar helps. Doesn't make any difference who the other woman is, but the better looking, the more that green-eyed monster rears its ugly head. Practice saying statements like, "Not sure I should show you this photo, but . . . ."

YOUR BROTHER-IN-LAW THINKS HE'S THE COOLEST GUY AROUND. HE'S ALWAYS TALKING ABOUT HIS WILD PARTIES AND HOW AWESOME HE IS AT HOSTING THEM. WHEN THE INVITE COMES FOR HIS CINCO DE MAYO SOIREE, IT'S YOUR TICKET TO SHUT HIM UP. . . .

MARGARITA MESS Ever washed a blender and then reassembled the parts incorrectly? There's a rubber seal that goes on top of the metal piece with the blades and just underneath the glass pitcher where everything gets blended. If you inadvertently place the seal in the wrong place, the pitcher leaks, leaving your Target one sloppy, sticky mess to clean up when he makes margaritas or any other blended drink. The trick is to place the rubber seal underneath the metal piece where the blades are attached so there is no seal to the glass pitcher. Your Target will wonder how he could be so stupid as to have made that mistake in the blender assembly.

THE BEER'S GONE FLAT With enough time and access, you drag his beer cases into the sun and bake them. If you only have access to his beer for a short time, then buy an

equal quantity of the same brand and let your beer bake. At the last minute, swap your baked suds for his good stuff. Nobody likes flat beer. To this day, there is one brand of beer I cannot drink because it sat on the sun-drenched Vietnam ship docks for weeks before it got to us First Air Cav troops up in the Central Highlands.

ANIMAL HOUSE Your Target has thrown a party that lasted late into the night. To assist his animal party image, you wait until he goes to bed, then quietly sneak over to his neighbor's house, the one he didn't invite to the party. Here, you toss a few rotten eggs on the porch. Leave a plain trail of footprints, broken eggs, and a couple of empty cans of the Target's favorite beer lead-

ing back to the Target's house. Prominently display an empty egg carton on your Target's front porch. The attacked neighbor will obviously be up first the next morning, see the mess, and draw his own conclusions.

There Was This One Time . . .

Here's an example of fitting revenge to opportunity. A friend, to remain unnamed, had the habit of staying out late and coming home drunk. His wife warned him, but he failed to listen. As a matter of late-night routine, he let himself into the house and stopped for a sandwich in the kitchen. He then enjoyed a smoke as he made his way to the bathroom to take a leak. Finished, he tossed the cigarette into the toilet and flushed. On this particular night, he ate his sandwich, lit his cigarette, took a leak, and tossed the cigarette as usual. *Boom!* Seems his wife had poured gasoline into the toilet bowl. The blast knocked him backward into the bathtub. He still drinks, but he is more careful about smoking.

SCENARIO

THAT'S IT. ENOUGH IS ENOUGH. YOU WERE NICE ENOUGH TO HOST THANKSGIVING DINNER AT YOUR HOME AND YOUR BROTHER AND SISTER-IN-LAW HAD THE AUDACITY TO MAKE A COMMENT ABOUT HOW BAD YOUR PLACE SMELLS. IT'S THEIR PLACE FOR CHRISTMAS, AND YOU'RE COMING WITH GIFTS. . . .

NESTERS There's something aesthetic and comfortable about the flicker of colorful flames in a wood-burning fireplace on a cold night. The flu has been opened to provide an updraft to keep the fire blazing and the logs are all well positioned. Everything is scenic and peaceful. Of course, you have previously scouted around until you located a large bird's nest, which you jammed into the top of the Target's chimney as if some birds had raised their young in that very location. Now, smoke from the fire-place stops rising up through the chimney. Instead, it backs up and fills the room where the wood-burning fireplace is located. That smell tends to stick around for several days.

FOLLOW YOUR NOSE Most couches, sofas, and easy chairs have a lightweight cloth stapled across the bottom. So, the next time you catch a small rodent in a mousetrap or find a recently deceased but still in good shape snake, scoop up the little critter. Then the next time you're in the Target's house, surreptitiously place the critter inside the couch or chair so it rests on top of that stapled cloth. You want a fresh specimen so it doesn't start smelling for a couple of days. When it does, he'll go nuts trying to locate the odor. He'll follow his nose and look under the couch, but he won't see anything there. And when he finally does find it, he'll start worrying about what hidden entrance the critter used to get inside the house.

DAMNING EVIDENCE It might not stink, but this will definitely smell fishy once it's planted and found by your sister-in-law. Obtain handwritten documents that show how your Target makes his cursive letters, or how he prints if that's how he writes. Practice writing the same way he does and with a ballpoint pen or a pencil, or whatever he typically uses. Purchase a little black address book. Fill the book with the first names of a few sexy-looking females he knows, plus several made-up names. Add in a rating system of up to five stars with some juicy comments for some of the names. Rub the book's outside, and make some erasures or cross-outs inside to make the book appear well used. Ensure his significant other finds this book somewhere in his possessions.

THE
HOME

ome, sweet home . . . it's such a warming phrase—most of the time. Here that's not really the case. This section is actually directed at the ladies, so they can take any necessary revenge on the significant other in their lives that's treated them wrong. The Ways go from mild to wild and depend on the temperament of the woman as well as the severity of her husband's or boyfriend's offense. Guys, you better watch out. This is the one time the attacker has open access to the Target. And that Target is *you*.

HE REALLY PISSED YOU OFF LAST NIGHT, GETTING INTO A HEATED BATTLE RIGHT BEFORE BED. NOW HE EXPECTS YOU TO GET UP EARLY AND GET HIS MORNING ROUTINE IN SWING. DON'T THINK SO . . . .

THAT WAS SOME CAFFEINE RUSH Many people like to have their morning coffee to start the day right. However, you can get his day off to a *real* quick start. Prepare the coffee like you would any morning, except that after you take your cup and before he takes his, add some liquid laxatives

to the pot. The first cup will get him going, and that second cup will have him running.

HEY, MY CEREAL MOVED Rice and granary weevils do not harm people or houses, and they do not bite, sting, or carry diseases. But these suckers are creepy. Picture your Target sitting down to breakfast. He pours cereal out of the box, adds milk, and as he's about to take a spoonful, he happens to notice his favorite cereal is moving. At this point, his appetite fades. These little pests develop inside whole-grain kernels as small white grublike larva that eat through the seed coat and emerge as adult weevils. They may appear in food seeds, popcorn, beans, garden seeds, decorative Indian corn, or any whole grain. Leave one of the listed foodstuffs sitting around long enough and you'll get yourselves some weevils. Keep them hidden until the time is right, then use them as instructed. They'll put him off his feed.

IT'S ONLY DONE ON ONE SIDE If your Target loves a nice slice of toast, buttered bagel, or English muffin in the morning, try this one. Root through the toolbox and find a pair of wire cutters. Next, go to the toaster. Pick a spot where the heating wires run close to an insulator. That's where you cut the heating element. His toast comes out brown only on one side; the other side is still as white and soft as when it came out of the package.

WARNING! Be sure the toaster is unplugged when you do the cutting, or you might light up like a Christmas tree.

SCENARIO

"HONEY, I JUST POPPED A BUTTON ON MY DRESS SHIRT. I'M RUNNING LATE. CAN YOU FIX IT? NOW?" SAID WITH NO CONSIDERATION OF HOW BUSY YOU ARE OR WHAT KIND OF SCHEDULE YOU ARE ON. SHOW HIM HOW HANDY YOU ARE WITH A NEEDLE AND THREAD. . . .

TAKE HIM DOWN TO SIZE If he's right-handed, shorten the left sleeve on all his long-sleeved shirts and lengthen the right sleeve if possible. One to two inches each should do it, just enough to throw him off kilter. Shorten one leg on all his pants, whether they are jeans, khakis, or suit pants. Once again, one to two inches—just make sure it's always the same side pants leg. Then watch as he constantly adjusts his pants at the waist to compensate for one

leg being shorter than the other. Let's see what your Target's final solution is. He'll know something's wrong in his world, but not what.

AS YE SEW If you know your sewing craft, then you know how to undo a factory-sewn stitch. So put this craft into practice and weaken some of the stitches in the seat of his dress slacks. Not so much that the weakened threads are visible when he puts on his pants, but enough that the seam will unravel with the pressure of him sitting down—preferably not his first sit down, but later in the day when he is well out of the house. He will then expose himself for the ass he really is. You may not see it in person, but you can bet you'll hear about this revealing moment.

HOW TO NEEDLE HIM You're having fun sewing and unsewing, but you'd really like to needle him some more, so find a thread color to match the underwear he puts on every day. Now sew shut the opening in the front of his underwear. The next time he pays a hurried visit to the men's room to relieve himself from all that coffee he drank at work or the copious quantities of beer consumed after work, he will quickly find it's difficult to get at his personal plumbing. In which case, he may have to spend some time in the restroom drying out, or else come home in ripped underwear.

YOU TOLD HIM THAT IF HE MADE ONE MORE COMMENT ABOUT THE NUMBER OF SHOES YOU OWN, HE'D REGRET IT. HE JUST DID. . . .

STRAIGHT AS A SNAKE Scoop up all his shoes and boots for either his right foot or his left foot. Only do one side. Take the footwear you selected to a shoe repair shop. Ask for a rush job, explaining that your boyfriend had an accident and now he needs one-inch taller heels on these shoes and boots. After the repairs, place the footwear back in his closet. The slightly taller heels will gradually make his spine curve out of line while he walks, and when his body tries to adjust to the unbalance, his spinal vertebrae will start to look like the snake he is. You'll know you succeeded when he complains of backaches.

SO TIGHT HE SQUEAKS The cheap SOB has money, but he never spends it on you. He drives an expensive car, but he never takes you out. Somehow you always end up cooking for him at your place, and he doesn't even spring for a bottle of wine. Now, the world needs to hear how tight he is. Locate his favorite leather shoes. Soak these shoes in water and dry them with a hair dryer. The adjoining pieces of leather dry at different rates, which will cause a loud squeaking when he walks. His first attempt to lessen the squeaking will involve him changing how his foot comes down when he steps. He may walk on the outside edge of his foot or the inner edge, or even do a heel-toe-hop to get rid of the irritating noise. Enjoy his funny new walk.

CLOWN SMILE Take a utility knife, or other very sharp but thin blade, and a pair of his best leather dress shoes. Insert the blade of the knife between the sole layers on the bottom of each shoe and slice the thread until most of the sole hangs loose. If the blade won't go in, you can try to cut the threads from outside on the bottom of the sole. Now use a cheap glue to stick the soles back into place. The next time he goes to work or a society event, his soles break loose and start flapping like clown shoes.

SCENARIO

EVERY MAN SHOULD KNOW THAT HE SHOULD NEVER, EVER MAKE A COMMENT ABOUT A WOMAN'S WEIGHT. IF HE'S NOT SMART ENOUGH TO KNOW THAT, THEN EXPOSE HIM FOR THE IDIOT HE IS. . . .

SHARP AS A RAZOR Take all of his belts to a hard flat surface where it's easy to cut leather with some amount of precision. Lay the belts one at a time on the cutting surface with the inside of the belt facing up. Now, using a razor or very sharp knife, slowly and carefully make a cut crosswise on the belt somewhere close to the buckle where it will be difficult to notice. Cut deep enough that the belt will eventually fall apart when placed under stress. Now there's nothing to hold up his pants, or his dignity.

IT'S A GROWING PROBLEM Write down an inventory of your Target's wardrobe. Then go shopping and buy the same brand, color, and style of shirts and pants he has in his closet, but buy them in both larger and smaller sizes. Substitute the larger size clothes that you bought. Remember to also substitute the tag that says what size the clothes are. Your Target thinks he can eat more, so be sure sweets and starchy foods come his way. When he grows into his new clothes, substitute his old clothes back into his wardrobe so he can feel the snugness. Mention a diet. Later, substitute the smaller size clothes you bought. He becomes frantic about his increasing size. Play with the settings on his weight scale.

OFF KILTER Your Target is a clotheshorse to which style and fashion are everything. So, take his suits out of the closet and get to work with scissors, needle, and thread. First, remove all the buttons from the front of his suit coat and then sew them back on an inch higher or lower than their original position. His altered suit coat now seems to hang out of synch with his intended image. He finds himself feeling off balance without knowing why. If the Target is a female, then do something similar with the buttons or fastenings on her dress clothes.

DO YOU HAVE THE FEELING WHEN HE COMES HOME LATE AT NIGHT WITH SOME LAME EXCUSE THAT MAYBE HE'S STRETCHING THE TRUTH? IT'S TIME TO TEACH HIM A LESSON. . . .

STRETCHING THINGS Take his underwear out of the dresser. It's your turn to stretch things. Pull on the elastic band of each pair of underpants until the elastic stretches out of shape, not so far as to be too visibly noticed, but enough that during his workday his underwear keeps drifting south. He'll find it's an irritant to constantly hike up his underwear, especially in public where he can't reach inside his pants to get a good grip on the cloth.

MAKE HIM BLUSH Throw a red sock and some bleach into his next load of tighty-whities. They'll come out a nice bright pink. You can bet he won't be wearing that particular under-wear to the gym or anyplace he has to change clothes. This also means that until he buys new underwear, he either goes com-mando or risks being gossiped about as the man in pink if he gets involved in an accident and ends up in the emergency room.

YOUR FLY'S OPEN Pick a pair of his pants, such as the slacks to one of his best suits, the suit he packs for important business trips. Remove the top stopper on the zipper so that the zipper comes off the track the next time he puts on his pants and pulls it all the way up. When he gets dressed for his meeting and the zipper comes apart, his fly is now open. He either has to dress down, buy a new suit on short notice, or try to come up with something to keep the side opposite of his ass from hanging out.

SOME ADVICE . . .

Your spouse keeps suddenly leaving the house to run unexpected errands, stays out later than usual, and is difficult to locate when you telephone where he said he was going. When you make inquiries later, he always has an excuse. Suspicion nags at your mind, but you have no proof anything's really going on. Well, don't bother to hire an expensive private eye. The SkyMall catalogue (*www.skymall.com*) will sell you a GPS tracking device for only $229.00. Hide the tracker in your vehicle, and the next time your spouse returns from one of those suspicious errands, merely replay his route to see where he really went.

THROUGH YOUR KEEN SKILLS OF OBSERVATION AND INTELLIGENCE RECON, AND HIS BLATANT STUPIDITY, YOU FIND OUT THAT HE HAS BEEN CHEATING ON YOU. OH, BOY . . . .

A BIRD IN THE HAND You're leaving the cheating SOB and never coming back, so put an inflatable doll in his bed as a parting gift. Never been inside an adult bookstore before?

Don't sweat it. Just explain to the clerk that your soon to be ex is a lousy lay, so you're leaving him something that doesn't care about lack of foreplay. The clerk will understand. He has heard it all, and may have some recommendations for this situation. Then, every time your ex looks into that plastic doll's blank staring eyes or sees those fake plastic breasts, he'll remember that warm, lively woman who's no longer around. When his friends find out about the blowup doll, they'll laugh and laugh. Double ouch.

HE'S NO BUTTERFLY This one takes timing, patience, and fast work. Put a set of thick, quality sheets on the bed, acquire some strong thread, and keep a large sewing needle handy. If your bully is a heavy drinker, then the next part is already done for you; otherwise, you may have to slip a couple of sleeping tablets into his last drink of the evening. When he's sound asleep, remove the top covers and loosen the bottom fitted sheet from around the mattress. Straighten out his legs and position his arms next to his body. Wrap the bottom sheet around him and sew the sheet from foot to head like he is in a cocoon. Pack your bags and leave. His coming-out process won't be easy, and there certainly won't be any beautiful transformation on his part.

THE SHORT OF IT Take his top sheet and his bottom sheet and sew them together crossways in the middle. Replace the sheets and make up the bed. When he crawls into bed that night his legs won't be able to straighten out because you short-sheeted him. When he pulls back the sheets to see the problem, he'll find a message you sewed to the new seam: "I always said you were *short*."

IF HE THINKS HE'S IN A STICKY SITUATION NOW, WAIT UNTIL HE FIGURES OUT WHAT YOU WERE UP TO BEFORE YOU LEFT HIS SORRY ASS. . . .

IT'S STUCK Most containers of superglue have an adequate quantity in the tube, so you're probably wondering where else you can apply this bonding agent in your Target's house. Just about everyone has a DVD player these days, and sooner or later a disk gets stuck in it or the player malfunctions with repeated use. Open the tray on the DVD player and insert his favorite DVD disk. Apply superglue to parts of the disk tray that make contact with other parts when the tray is closed. Close the tray. Who's to say it wasn't a regular malfunction? If he wants his favorite DVD disk, he'll have to pry it out.

DAMN CHEAP FOREIGN CAMERAS Find that digital camera your Target's so proud of. Claims he really got a bargain. Too bad the rest of you suckers aren't as quick as he is. Turn on the camera's power and zoom out the lens. Liberally apply glue to the sides of the lens. Now zoom the lens back in, turn off the power, and put the camera back where you found it. The next time he goes to take a distant shot, his lens won't budge and he'll start thinking maybe his bargain wasn't so good after all.

THE NEVER-ENDING WAKE-UP Go to his radio alarm clock, which is set to automatically wake him with his favorite music. Readjust the alarm time for two hours earlier and change the radio station to a fire-and-brimstone preacher. Raise the volume to peak level. Glue the knobs and switches to all your new settings. When his alarm blasts him out of bed, he'll have to unplug or break the radio to shut it up, and the loss of two hours sleep will make his day drag.

SCENARIO

HOLD ON, I'M GONNA SNEEZE You know your Target has allergic reactions to dogs and cats. So, you've collected several hairs from whichever animal is the problem—just in case. Now is the time to scatter these hairs between his sheets and inside his pillowcases. His eyes will water every night and his nose will run constantly, but since he has no animals as pets, he won't figure out where the problem is.

ACHOO: PART 2 Pollen tends to be the other major aggravator of allergies. If that's the case with your Target, you can exacerbate the problem. Ragweed in the summer and fall, and the yellow pollen of pine trees in the spring, are good ones to gather. These pollens can be spread in his bedroom, his clothes drawer or closet, the interior of his vehicle so that the car's heater or air conditioner blow the pollen around in the vehicle's closed environment, or you can dust the surfaces in his workplace so he can't concentrate on his job. Stand by with a box of tissues so it appears you are in sympathy with his problem, but cover that smile and try not to laugh.

IT WAS GIGANTIC If you have some time and a few extra bucks, buy a couple of big Mexican tarantulas from a pet store. I'm talking about the red-kneed tarantula. It has a dark-colored, hairy abdomen. Its characteristic legs have orange to dark red-orange joints and some smaller patches of orange on the legs. He is one of the most docile species available in captive collections, but your Target won't know that. Turn the tarantulas loose in his bedroom where they will hopefully crawl across his face while he is sleeping. The worse that will happen, other than becoming afraid to sleep at night, is the tarantula, when agitated, will occasionally flick barb-like hairs at an offender, which can cause irritation or blistering.

WARNING! If the tarantula's hairs hit the Target's eyes, it can cause vision damage.

POTTY TRAINING Sure, it's an old trick, but it still works. Raise the lid and the seat on the toilet in his bathroom. Then take a large roll of cellophane wrap and stretch it across the top of his porcelain bowl. Use more than one sheet if necessary to completely cover the bowl opening, but just make sure there are no visible wrinkles in the cellophane or loose ends showing. The next time he stands there to take a leak, he's gonna have one of those accidents much the same as if he had bad aim.

SLIPPING AND A SLIDING Go into the bathroom and apply a nice coat of wax to the floor of his shower or tub. Rub it in good so no residue visibly gives away the free house-cleaning work you just performed. You can apply wax to the entire shower/tub floor, or you can select a certain area, say the back of the shower or one end of the tub so he's completely inside before the skating starts, or apply the wax in stripes to provide a skid, brake, skid, brake scenario. Just be aware that any falls could result in injuries to your Olympic tub skater.

ROTO-ROOTER MAN Take a sanitary napkin, the larger the better, and flush it down his toilet. Now flush another one and another one and keep going until the toilet bowl doesn't clear anymore. Stop before the bowl overflows. Leave that particular present for him to enjoy.

> **WARNING!** If he has one of those modern toilets—which advertise that they can flush a cantaloupe—this trick may not work very well until the sewer pipes themselves get clogged.

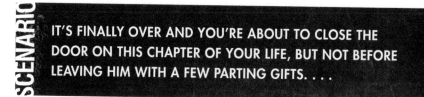

SCENARIO

IT'S FINALLY OVER AND YOU'RE ABOUT TO CLOSE THE DOOR ON THIS CHAPTER OF YOUR LIFE, BUT NOT BEFORE LEAVING HIM WITH A FEW PARTING GIFTS. . . .

DISAPPEARING CARD TRICK You saw it coming in time, so you set up your own checking account and credit cards. You may have been battered emotionally, but financially you can keep on going, knowing full well that he would fight you to the last penny before he gave you anything. Now it's time for him to think about that last penny thing. As you depart, you quietly cut up all his credit and debit cards and throw the

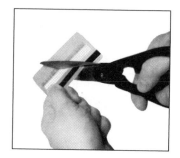

pieces in the bottom of the trashcan. He won't know if they were lost or stolen. Also shred his checkbook and files of monthly bank statements. In today's cashless society, people depend upon their cards for purchases. It takes several days to replace these cards.

SIR, THE POLICE ARE COMING If you're leaving the house and not coming back due to divorce or a hostile splitting of the sheets, get your hands on the house alarm manual. Look up the section for changing the access code. Follow the instructions and change the code to numbers he will never guess. Set the alarm and leave. The next time he enters the residence, he won't be able to silence the raucous noise. The alarm company will call for the verbal password to shut off the system, but hey, you can always call them and change that too before you leave. He'll have fun talking with the cops late that night, especially if he has a temper and has been out drinking for several hours.

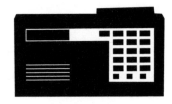

THE NUMBERS GAME On your way out the door, you stop with one foot in the house and one foot in the garage. What else can you do to get the last word? Your fingers tap the wall next to the doorway. Oh yeah, the garage door opener. He's got a remote control inside his car, so you toss his remote into your vehicle. Unscrew the plastic cover on the door opener button inside the garage, cut the wires, and replace the cover. Then you read the manual on how to change the code numbers on the outside keypad. Anytime he wants his car in or out of the garage, he'll have to lift and lower the door manually—that lazy SOB.

LOCATION 7

ON

VACATION

You've been looking forward to your vacation for months now. The pressure of work has got you stressed, or maybe you needed time away to figure out some of the problem points in your relationship with someone special. Whatever the reason you had for getting out of town for a few days, the chance for relaxation without any friction is just what the doctor ordered for you to get your head straight again. But, as you settle into a comfortable lounge chair, the outside world finds a piece of you and there is no peace in your world.

SCENARIO

YOU'RE CALMLY SEATED AT A RESORT OR IN SOME TOURIST ATTRACTION JUST ENJOYING THE VIEW WHEN ALL HELL BREAKS LOOSE. YOU DON'T NECESSARILY KNOW WHO OR WHAT STARTED THE RUCKUS, BUT IT LOOKS LIKE SOMEONE IS ABOUT TO MAKE YOU PART OF IT. A GUY COMES RUSHING STRAIGHT AT YOU WITH HIS FIST DRAWN BACK . . . .

WELL SEATED You don't want this to be a bad end to your vacation, so with both hands you grab the sides of your chair for good balance and get ready. When he gets close enough, you kick straight out into his solar plexus with your shoe. *OOF!* While he's trying to catch his breath, you pay your bill and depart the premises before the cops arrive. It's your vacation; you don't want to waste your time filling out police reports.

GO ON THE DEFENSIVE: The Jujitsu Block

You may be on vacation having a nice, peaceful time, but you never know when some clown will decide to pick a fight, and you're his intended meat. If you are in a situation where you see that a punch will be coming in your direction, you may want to consider a jujitsu method of blocking a punch. Step in close to your attacker and throw both arms up to the inside of his forearms or elbows. Any incoming punch will now travel to the outside and be harmless. This is a good time to switch to a karate strike with your hand or foot. Or, you can use one of the judo or jujitsu throws previously mentioned if you're close enough and in a good position to utilize them.

SPOONING ANKLE THROW Use your left hand to grab the back of his left elbow from the inside. Pull left so he ends up turning almost sideways to you. Bend your left knee and lean your upper body forward while placing your right hand on his left shoulder and hooking your right foot behind his left ankle. Now, simultaneously pull left with your left hand, push backward on his left shoulder, and use your right foot to sweep his left ankle to your left and upward. He'll fall like a rotten tree.

Jujitsu: The term comes from *jiu*, "gentle, pliable," and *jitsu*, "art or science." By utilizing psychological techniques, anatomy, and skills obtained through practice rather than brute strength, it erases differences in height, weight, or arm length between you and your opponent. Although it shares many common throws and movements with judo, jujitsu is not a sport.

PRESSURE ON KNEE FRONT THROW If you're going to try this one, you'd best have quick reflexes. Let's assume you're in a position where you know circumstances are rapidly deteriorating and will soon become physical. Not wanting to be injured by some out-of-control tourist who has decided that his vacation stinks and he's going to make someone else pay for it, you decide to act first. Stepping forward, you smear your palm over his nose. In surprise, he leans back. You quickly drop to your left knee, place your right forearm just above the kneecap of whichever foot

he has forward, and your left hand grabs behind the ankle of this forward foot. Then, pressing back hard with your right forearm, you pull toward yourself and up with your left hand. He'll fall backward. Be careful in practice because this move can fracture the knee.

SCENARIO

YOU'RE STANDING AT THE COUNTER PATIENTLY WAITING YOUR TURN TO PURCHASE AN OVERPRICED GOLF JACKET FROM THIS GIFT STORE YOU'VE WANDERED INTO WHEN A PUSHY TOURIST GIVES YOU THE ELBOW AND CROWDS IN FRONT. WHEN YOU PROTEST THAT HE'S STEPPED ON TOP OF YOUR SHOE AND HE REALLY OUGHT TO WAIT IN LINE, HE GIVES YOU A SCORNFUL LOOK AND A FEW NASTY COMMENTS. . . .

THE OLD PENCIL TRICK You don't want a fist fight, so you pick up one of the pens or pencils lying on the counter and position this pencil between your index and middle finger all the way back against the web of your hand. Now, grab his wrist with your free hand, slide the pencil between any two of his fingers, and squeeze his hand tightly with your pencil hand. The pain resulting from the pencil pressing against two of his finger bones will make him suddenly more polite.

I'VE GOT A LOADED JACKET Take a lesson from the early 1900 Parisian street gangs called apaches (pronounced *ah-PAHASH*): When carrying a jacket or coat across their

arm or over their shoulder, they would suddenly thrust it with both hands at their opponent and over his head, thus blocking his vision. And while their opponent was temporarily blinded, they commenced to batter his head, face, and body. Remember, he who strikes first *and hard* usually wins in a street confrontation.

LOADED JACKET: PART 2 You can also take a lesson from the savate instructors of that time who used common articles of clothing to develop defenses against these apache gangsters. The instructor's use of the jacket was to place heavy items such as coins in the pockets of his jacket. When the instructor was confronted by street hoodlums, he would swing or whip the jacket like a club. The weight in the pocket acted as an extended blackjack. Slip whatever you have in your pants pockets into the pocket of the jacket. A heavy key ring, several coins, a camera. Yeah, I know, cameras cost money, but then compare that small cost to the price of doctor bills these days, plus the pain of taking a beating. To heck with the camera. Now throw in a few kicks to his kneecaps and groin while you're still ticked off about maybe having to damage your camera.

There Was This One Time . . .

A blackjack, illegal in most places, is a round, spring-loaded weight sewn into a leather covering, whereas a head slapper has a flat weight. Use either one too hard and they bust the Target's skull. On the other hand, don't count on these weapons putting the Target down. I speak from personal experience. While protecting an asset late one night, a member of the other side saw fit to suddenly employ a blackjack to my forehead. It knocked me back but not down, whereupon, I drew my automatic from the back of my waistband and they scattered. Had it not been for blood running down into my eyes, I'd have blown a hole in the direction of my attackers and taken my chances on scoring. However, had I missed, a civilian eating pancakes at a nearby restaurant would have had the surprise of his life. I don't recommend these objects.

SCENARIO

YOU'RE HAVING FUN AT YOUR VACATION RESORT, NOT BOTHERING ANYONE ELSE, AND ALL OF A SUDDEN YOU BUMP THE PATIO TABLE NEXT TO YOU AND SPILL A GUY'S BEER. HE DOESN'T ACCEPT YOUR APOLOGY AND YOUR OFFER TO BUY HIM A FRESH BEER. INSTEAD, HE GETS TOUGH TO IMPRESS HIS BUDDIES. IT LOOKS LIKE FISTICUFFS, AND HE'S BIGGER THAN YOU. . . .

THE GAME'S A FOOT Now's another time to consider the use of savate, a form of foot fighting developed by French sailors about 300 years ago. Using your leg closest to your opponent, kick his shin with the instep of your shoe in a sweeping motion. Obviously, this works best if you are wearing hard-soled shoes instead of flip-flops. The sharp edge of your shoe's instep will remove one of the two legs he needs to stand on if he wishes to pursue the issue any further.

FIGHTING STYLE

Savate: A French martial art in which the hands and feet are used in a combination of boxing and kicking techniques.

THE BELT DROP In the martial art of judo, there's a tactic called the Belt Drop. It is seldom used in tournaments because the movements used to set it up are obvious to another trained competitor. However, when the proper opportunity presents itself, the tactic works quite well. When your opponent is standing straight up and facing you, slide your left hand up under the front of his belt. Immediately slam your right forearm into his throat while pulling toward you on his belt with your left hand, and positioning your right leg behind and against the back of his calves. He will be forced up on his toes and his upper body will be leaning far backward. He's now suspended. Step your right leg back to drop him.

BUCKLE UP Got caught empty-handed? Reach down to your waist, undo that belt, and yank it out of the belt loops. Wrap the belt around your hand a couple of times so it stays locked in place. Leave the buckle end out. You have just fashioned a weapon to whip across the attacker's eyes. If you wear one of those large Western buckles, they usually have a small metal hook on the underside. The weight of a hard-swung Western buckle on the far end of your belt can cause nasty damage to an attacker as can the small metal hook on the underside. Just make sure your pants won't fall down.

SOME ADVICE . . .

You can't take a knife or a gun on an airplane when you travel, and handgun permits usually aren't valid in any state other than where you got that permit. But, you also know that somewhere along your trip, you may pass through a questionable section of the country. So what's a nice, legal weapon to carry along for protection? Why, a walking cane of course. If someone looks at you funny, just limp a little to make it appear as though it is a normal object for you to be carrying. Yes, you can purchase fighting canes or sword canes, but you don't want one of them in hand for the cops to examine if you have to clobber an assailant. I've worked some registered bull sales in my time, so my cane came from a livestock feed store. It's strong, inexpensive, and looks ordinary.

SCENARIO

YOU'RE WALKING THROUGH THE STREETS OF A NOT-SO-FRIENDLY NEIGHBORHOOD WHILE VISITING ONE OF THOSE NOT-SO-FRIENDLY COUNTRIES. A MUGGER JUMPS OUT FROM AN ALLEY WITH A KNIFE DRAWN AND THREATENS YOUR LIFE. LUCKY FOR YOU, YOU BROUGHT YOUR TRUSTY CANE. . . .

A FLICK OF THE WRIST The rubber tip of the cane is resting on the ground and you've reversed the cane's handle so your hand is gripping the short end of the crook, which is facing forward. Your body weight exerts a slight pressure down on the cane. When your opponent approaches close enough, merely flick your wrist to flip the rubber end of the cane up into the enemy's groin. The sudden release of your downward pressure on the cane adds a springing momentum to your delivery. You may now use the rubber tip of the cane in a spearing motion or the crook as a hammer to further disable your attacker. When you're finished, he may need his own cane to walk upright in the future.

TO HOOK A CROOK A cane has two ends, so be prepared to utilize either end. If you are seated or have been knocked to the ground, you'll find the crook end of the cane makes a convenient hook to catch the ankle of a fleeing criminal, and thus trip him up. And yes, while he is temporarily stunned by his fall, apply either end of your hard wood stick to keep him down. Many times in battle, the first blow decides the winner. If you are in a standing position, use the crook end to catch the fleeing criminal around the throat and yank him to an abrupt halt. As one of our famous past presidents said, "Walk softly and carry a big stick." I wonder if he had all this in mind.

DISARMING YOUR TARGET By making a slight alteration in the above movements, you have the ability to disarm any opponent attacking you with his knife held at waist level. In this case, instead of flipping your cane up into his groin, you can flip the cane's hard shaft up into the bones of his knife wrist or forearm. If you do it hard enough and fast enough, his knife will go flying. Once again, follow up by utilizing the tip as a spear or the crook as a hammer to render your attacker hors de combat. Should you find yourself in dire circumstances with little choice, this same action will work against an opponent carrying a handgun; however, since the gun may discharge anyway, be sure to move your body to one side and out of the line of fire as you strike.

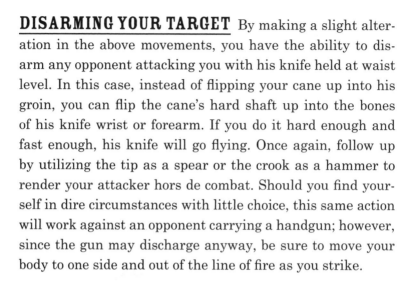

SCENARIO

YOU'RE WALKING THROUGH THE AIRPORT HEADED FOR YOUR DEPARTURE GATE WHEN YOU SEE THAT GUY WHO WAS GIVING EVERYONE A HARD TIME AT THE SECURITY CHECKPOINT. HE EVEN SHOVED AN ELDERLY WOMAN OUT OF THE WAY WHEN HE WENT TO GET HIS THINGS FROM THE X-RAY CONVEYOR BELT. NOW, HE'S UP AT THE WINDOW GAZING OUT AT THE AIRCRAFT WHILE HIS CARRY-ON BAG SITS BEHIND HIM IN A WAITING-AREA SEAT. . . .

NO TICKEE, NO RIDE There in plain sight is his boarding pass sticking out of a suitcase pocket. You stroll over to the adjoining seat and casually drop your jacket so part of it covers his boarding pass. Suddenly, you remember somewhere you have to be and grab your jacket. The boarding pass surreptitiously comes with it as you walk away. No doubt he'll be fun at the loading gate.

HAIRY IDEAS Here's an exotic one for all you nature and scientific types. It's the urticating hair of the saddleback caterpillar. These hairs are the caterpillar's defense system. And they can be your method of offense. Human contact with urticating hairs causes skin reactions such as inflammation, rashes, and itching. Enough hairs can turn a person's entire torso red. Either go out in the woods and collect a few of these twitchy guys, or hit up the Internet and purchase them through a specialty site. No matter how you go about procuring them, be careful not to get caught leaving them in your Target's bed.

KNOW THE LINGO

URTICATE
To cause a stinging or itching sensation.

THE BIG BANG THEORY You discovered some old fireworks you failed to shoot off the last Fourth of July, and there's still several months to go until the next chance to legally light them up. What to do with these black powder items? Well, here's an idea. Break open these pyrotechnics and spread the powder inside the suitcase of your Target. The small black grains will be easily missed the next time he packs that suitcase for an airline flight. However, when airport security detects the powder, they will pull him out of line to answer a few questions while they give his bag another look. Of course, he won't have any answers.

LOCATION 8

THE
NEIGHBORHOOD

Mr. Rogers doesn't live here. . . . Sometimes you get a good neighborhood where everyone gets along, all the neighbors look out for the other residents, and families don't have to worry about their kids playing in the yard. But sometimes your neighborhood is or has gradually degenerated into an unfriendly enclave of warring clans. Neighbors don't speak to each other, unless it's to raise their voice in accusation or complaints about where you park your car, kids playing basketball in your driveway, or the TV satellite mounted on the side of your garage roof, the only location you can get good reception. The neighbors are slowly grinding away at your quality of everyday life, and you're tired of their unreasonableness.

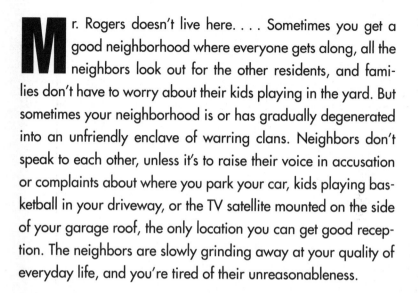

SCENARIO

YOUR FAT, BEER-SWILLING, HUMONGOUS NEIGHBOR GOT PISSED ABOUT SOMETHING AND NOW HE'S GETTING PHYSICAL. ALL YOU WERE DOING WAS CLEANING OUT YOUR GARAGE, BUT WITH THE RAGE HE'S EXHIBITING, YOU COULD GET SERIOUSLY INJURED. . . .

I'M GONNA ROCK YOUR WORLD If you're near a decorative landscaped yard when trouble starts, look around for a nice rock. Them pretty little pebbles won't do you much good, and, unless you've kept up with your weight training, that big boulder will only provide you with a hernia. Color and whatever minerals the rock is made out of don't count at this point; however, the right size and gripability does, so select one you can get your hand around. Oh, and remember to keep your fingers from getting between the rock and your intended Target. Broken or bent fingers make for an awkward second swing.

I DIG YA Shovels have an easy-to-grip handle with a curved metal weight at the opposite end. They can be employed as a bat, cutting device, or unpadded pugil stick. For those of you lacking military service, a pugil stick, padded on either end, is held with both hands in a crosswise position across your body. Two trainees, facing each other, swing the top end of the stick to knock the other guy's head off, or use the bottom end in a butt stroke to engage the other's groin or chin. And, if the situation goes wrong, you now have a burying tool.

WARNING! Permanently removing your opponent is not the object of this excise. Homicide charges will ruin your day.

IF I HAD A HAMMER Hammers are tools found in most homes. I have personally opened many a door with a sledgehammer, plus used a standard claw hammer to pound buckets of nails in rough frame construction. The ball-peen hammer is normally utilized to shape metal and rivets. And the Hells Angels must have a lot of metal to shape on their customized scooters, since some of them have taken to carrying ball-peen hammers in their back pockets. Of course, on the surface, if you've got a ball-peen hammer or a crescent wrench in your back pocket, people naturally assume you have a repair project somewhere. It's not like you're toting a gun or knife out in public. But, why do you think they carry them?

SOME ADVICE . . .

Many new vehicles have three buttons above the front windshield that can be coded to open a garage door. More than likely you've set one of these buttons to open your own garage door, which leaves you with two do-nothing buttons. Of course, if you had the time, read the manual on how the Target's brand of garage door opener worked, and had a couple of minutes access for one reason or other, you could always train one of your do-nothing buttons to open your Target's garage door. Now you have access whenever you need it. Just remember that other neighbors sometimes get nosey.

THAT JERK THINKS HE CAN ATTACK YOU IN YOUR OWN GARAGE? YOU ALREADY SHOWED HIM ONCE, BUT YOU MIGHT AS WELL DRIVE HOME THE POINT BY MESSING AROUND WITH THE STUFF IN HIS GARAGE. . . .

THEY DON'T MAKE THEM LIKE THEY USED TO

Using a fine saw blade, cut the wooden handles on all your Target's tools. Make the cut where the wood enters or meets the metal part of the tool. Only cut partway through. Now fill the incision with wood putty to conceal the cut. Stain the putty to match the wooden handle. The next time your Target decides to drive a nail, the hammer head will fall off. When he applies pressure to his shovel handle, it will come apart at the blade. Rakes will snap, sledgehammers will bend, and he will end up holding a long piece of worthless wood. His projects will always be behind schedule.

LOOKS LIKE OIL Get access to your Target's lawn mower. Raise one end of the mower body and block it with a couple of paint cans or something so you can work underneath. Find the correct size socket to fit the oil drain plug on the bottom of the mower. Loosen the plug far enough that it doesn't leak but will eventually vibrate loose. At some point in mowing his nice green lawn, the drain plug will fall out, leaving a black trail of drops at first, then a solid wet line, and finally a dark puddle when he stops to research the problem. In a few days, those oil drips, lines, and puddles lead to dead, brown grass. So much for a beautiful lawn.

DAMN PIECE OF TRASH Find a spot on your Target's lawn mower where the pull start cord crosses through or over a piece of metal, a place that looks like it could be a natural rub spot. Use a metal file to work on the cord in that likely rub spot. File all around the cord until it appears ready to break after a few more starts. When the cord finally comes apart, allegedly through normal wear, he won't be able to trim the lawn when he expected to have time for this job. Now he has to decide whether to buy a new lawn mower or try to get the old one fixed. Either way it costs him money and his lawn keeps getting more unsightly. Notify the Homeowners Association.

There Was This One Time . . .

I knew a guy back east who played in poker games arranged by the mafia. He studied their routine, then sent a friend to the local drug store where mafia runners bought their playing cards. His friend acquired all the card decks in their favorite brand. The guy steamed open the cellophane on each package and marked the cards. The cards went back into the boxes, got resealed, and his friend did a reverse shoplift by placing the marked decks back on the drugstore's shelves. That night, the guy made it a point to lose and keep asking for a new deck. When the dealer was down to his last one, the guy ripped it up in mock rage at losing again, then apologized and gave the runner twenty bucks to go down to the drugstore and buy new decks. He kicked poker ass the rest of the night.

SOME ADVICE . . .

Your neighbors are up to something, but you don't know what. You catch them looking toward your house and whispering behind their hands so you can't read their lips. Well, you can find out what they're up to and be ready for their next move. Your favorite airline's SkyMall catalogue lists an electronic listening device for only $59.95. It's powerful enough to capture sounds up to 300 feet, and like the real spies, you can even record their conversation. Having now confirmed your neighbors have no intention of doing you a good turn daily, you can, as the Boy Scouts say, "Be prepared."

SCENARIO

WHO DOES YOUR NEIGHBOR THINK HE IS, COMPLAINING ABOUT THE NUMBER OF CARS IN YOUR DRIVEWAY? IT'S YOUR HOUSE, YOUR DRIVEWAY, AND YOUR CARS. TEACH HIM THAT HE SHOULD MIND HIS OWN PROPERTY, IF HE'S REALLY THAT INTERESTED. . . .

CRACKING UP Got a good friend who drives large dump trucks for a heavy construction outfit? Excellent. On one of his runs, when his truck is fully loaded with chunks of concrete or gravel, have him motor over to the Target's house, back into his cement drive, then pull out forward and drive off in the opposite direction from which he came. Nothing gets dumped in the drive, and to any casual observer it merely looks as if the dump truck turned around because he was going the wrong way. What really happens is the weight of the loaded truck causes the Target's driveway cement to start cracking. As time goes by, the alternating freezing and thawing widens the cracks.

TOTALLY INSURED You've got two problems. First, your car is getting old and needs a paint job, but you don't have money available. Second, your neighbor has a large tree on his side of the property with a huge limb that hangs over your driveway. You've spoken to him about the heavy branch, but he won't do anything about it. So, when it gets dark, you girdle the base of that branch with a length of wire and you keep your old car parked underneath the branch. As the limb grows, it weakens at the wire girdle. Eventually, a big storm will break the branch, which falls on your car roof. His insurance pays off.

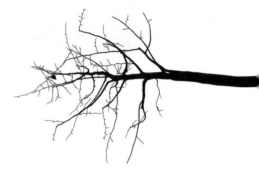

I'D LIKE TO REPORT MY NEIGHBOR Late at night, on several different occasions, drive into your Target's driveway in a friend's car with the stereo blaring music. Sit in the driveway long enough to slam the car doors a couple of times, so it sounds like someone is getting in and out of the vehicle. Leave, and come back later in a different car. Repeat the same scenario with the music and doors. Obviously, you can stay in his driveway longer if you know the Target is not home. Eventually, the neighbors will suspect he's a drug dealer with lots of traffic. They will start treating him differently and may even call in a report to the police.

YOUR NEIGHBOR KEEPS REMOVING THE POLITICAL SIGN YOU HAVE POSTED IN FRONT OF YOUR HOUSE DURING ELECTION TIME. YOU'VE GONE OVER TO SPEAK WITH HIM A NUMBER OF TIMES NOW, BUT HE KEEPS DOING IT— SOMETHING ABOUT HOW SIGNS DEPRECIATE PROPERTY VALUE. WELL, HIS VALUE IS ABOUT TO BE DEPRECIATED. . . .

SLIPPERY POLITICIANS It's that time of year where politicians flood the airwaves with ads and get their supporters to place political signs in their front yards. These supporters are the type of people who get emotionally involved with the candidate of their party, and they tend to take offense at any slight to their choice. So, all you do is remove the political signs from their yard and leave a visible trail of damaged signs leading back to the Target's nearby house where the rest of the "stolen" signs can be easily found, barely concealed in his bushes out front. The retaliations begin.

FOR SALE Wait until one of his neighbors is having a garage sale on a weekend. You remove all the sale signs and

leave a trail of broken wood and poster board leading over to his house in the same manner as the Way above, which will definitely not endear him to his outraged neighbor who went to a lot of trouble to have the sale.

OR TRY THIS! Plant the garage sale sign in the Target's yard and let him deal with the garage sale buyers who keep ringing his doorbell on a Saturday morning while he's trying to sleep in late.

ANYONE HOME? Really feel like pissing him off? Go around town and post Open House fliers on telephone poles and streetlights. You'll have all sorts of people showing up at your neighbor's home, expecting to get a walkthrough. Heck, some might even just walk right in. It is an Open House after all. You could take this one step further and post the Open House on online sites that host sales by homeowners.

WARNING! If you choose to go the online route, be sure to make the posting from a public computer. Authorities will be able to trace the posting to your personal computer.

YOU JUST DON'T LIKE THIS GUY. HE'S A COMPLETE SLEAZE. IT'S ABOUT TIME THE REST OF THE NEIGHBORHOOD FELT THE SAME WAY YOU DO. . . .

THAT PIECE OF TRASH Wait until your Target puts his trash out at the curb and goes to work. Now, walk up to his trashcan and place an old inflatable sex doll with a couple of patches on it into his trash. Be sure the doll hangs out enough to be recognized for what it is by all the neighbors. If you don't know any perverts who have an old doll you can "borrow," then man up and go to your local adult store and purchase one. Rub some dirt and baby oil on the doll so it looks well used. The neighbors will quickly form their own opinion about him.

THE LOCAL PORNO KING You've located someone's stash of pornographic magazines. Of course, they're not yours, but you know just the place to get rid of them. On your Target's trash day, after he's put out the garbage cans and gone to work, you come by and drop off the magazines in a stack next to his trashcans. To maximize the results, you enact this plan on a windy day so the magazines will blow into the neighbors' yards and hang up in their bushes. To point the accusing finger of shame in the right direction, you have placed mailing labels with his name and address on the cover of each magazine. Neighborhood relationships won't be the same.

GNOME HOME Is there someone in the Target's neighborhood suffering from the loss of lawn ornaments in the dead of night? Pick up some of those remaining portable lawn decorations, transfer said decorations to the front yard of Target's house, and take photos. Ensure the house number shows up. Return the items, but hide them under the owner's bushes where they won't be found for a while. You know what to do with the photos. Sit back and watch. Since the items were returned, you technically haven't stolen them, and when the owners find them later, they will think your Target got cold feet after he was found out and therefore brought them back.

SOME ADVICE . . .

Once trash is put out at the curb, it is generally considered to be "abandoned property." This is when cops and private investigators go through their Target's trash to see what they can find out about him. What you do is find documents with his name and address on them, remove these bags of trash, and take them with you. These bags now need to find their way to the front steps of the mayor's office building or the property of some city official who is a firebrand or under pressure for one of his decisions. They will take this trash as a personal affront and investigate who the trash belongs to. Think they will believe his protestations of innocence?

SCENARIO

THAT GUY ACTUALLY HAD THE AUDACITY TO CALL THE POLICE ON YOU? BECAUSE OF A BARBECUE YOU THREW ON A SATURDAY AFTERNOON? SHOW HIM WHAT HAPPENS WHEN THERE'S AN ACTUAL REASON TO GET THE AUTHORITIES INVOLVED. . . .

THE HOA POLICE If your Target lives in a Homeowners Association neighborhood, find out what the covenants are. The stricter, the better. No doubt, you've heard in the news how nasty some of these HOA board of directors can get when they find a violator in their midst. And, I'm sure you can use these same covenants to help your Target become a violator subject to escalating fines, which if not paid soon lead to a lien against the Target's house. Anonymously sent photos of the violation will get that HOA board moving. Some violations are as easy as growing weeds or an unmowed lawn.

THINKING A HEAD Can you keep your lunch down? Good. Borrow your Target's hunting knife that everyone recognizes or a large carving knife from a set in his kitchen. Wear gloves. Check the roadsides for a fresh road kill deer. Cut off the head and wrap it in plastic. Place the deer head and knife in a partly concealed place in his backyard. Sounds like the horse head scene out of *The Godfather*, doesn't it? For an added twist, place an anonymous call about a possible poacher. If your call turns out to be traceable and the police come knocking on your door, merely explain you were driving by and saw someone carrying a deer head into his backyard. Be vague in your description, and don't be so lamebrained as to describe yourself.

GONE TO POT   Gather up *cannabis sativa L.* seeds, otherwise known as marijuana. Spread these seeds over your Target's lawn and garden, or sew them in out-of-the way places where he is likely to overlook them. In the first instance, his neighbors suspect him of criminal activities; otherwise, where did the seeds come from? In the second instance, you make an anonymous call to the authorities to report this giant illegal plant in his backyard. A note of caution about gathering these seeds: possession of them is a crime in some states. Plus, if you gather them in the wild, you risk meeting law enforcement who assume you're harvesting your own grow operation, or you might even meet an outraged grower who thinks you're stealing his money crop.

SCENARIO

YOU BOUGHT A HOUSE FOR THE TERRIFIC VIEW, BUT YOUR NEIGHBOR SUBSEQUENTLY PLANTED A LARGE TREE THAT BLOCKED IT. YOU HAD POLITELY ASKED IF HE WOULD PLANT THE TREE IN A DIFFERENT PLACE, BUT THE JERK DIDN'T CARE ABOUT YOUR PROBLEM, AND HIS LIP EVEN CURLED UP IN A SMIRK. A FEW YEARS HAVE PASSED, THE TREE HAS GROWN, AND YOUR SCENIC VIEW HAS SHRUNK. . . .

CAN'T SEE THE FOREST

It's late at night, you've got your dark commando gear on, and you holstered your best cordless drill, preferably loaded with a small drill bit. Sticking to the shadows, you alligator crawl across your Target's front lawn to a tree blocking his view of the street. Zip, you drill six or eight holes slanting down into the trunk of the tree. Whipping out a convenient syringe filled with herbicide, you inject each hole. Several days later, you walk by his house. He's out front with a chain saw, complaining to other neighbors that some kind of bug has bored into his tree and killed it.

KNOW THE LINGO

ALLIGATOR CRAWL

With your head down and stomach on the ground, move your left leg and right arm forward. Keep your right leg and left arm straight. Then move forward with your right leg and left arm, keeping your left leg and right arm straight. Repeat until you get to where you want to go.

THE GIRDLE We're back to that damn tree in your neighbor's yard, the large tree he planted to block your scenic view. You'd like to get rid of it, but running across the street in the dead of night to fire up a chain saw and yell "timber" isn't feasible. No, something quiet and stealthy is more appropriate. Maybe something you could anticipate and enjoy for months to come. So one dark night, you dash across the street with a piece of thin wire and twist said wire tightly around the tree trunk. As the tree grows, the wire weakens its superstructure. Come a high wind and you won't have to yell "timber," it will just fall.

TENTING TONIGHT There's a little black caterpillar called a tent worm. These guys erupt into colonies covered by silk- or weblike threads, hence the name tent worms. By the time they get established and lay eggs, all the tree or bush leaves inside the "tent" have been eaten down to the bark. The worms then move on to the next branch or tree, and can completely kill their host. The remedy is to spray the tree with pesticide, which costs money. In the meantime, your Target's stripped tree is an eyesore in the neighborhood and all his neighbors will be complaining because they don't want their trees to become infected with the same plague.

SOME ADVICE . . .

One of the problems of actions you take inside his house is acquiring access to the residence. Damaging a door or window is breaking and entering. And even if you found the door unlocked, in some states the mere act of physically crossing the plane of the doorway is considered a felony. Besides possibly gaining access through the garage using the aforementioned garage-opener trick, there are usually unlocked windows and already-torn screens that small objects can be inserted through. Or, if you're a good talker, you can scam your way in for a few minutes under some pretext. Use your imagination. In my twenty-five years of working undercover, I was frequently surprised by what ideas worked on the idiots of the opposing team.

THAT'S IT. THE GUY NEXT DOOR HAS FINALLY PUSHED YOUR BUTTONS ENOUGH TO THE POINT WHERE YOU'VE SNAPPED. YOU NEED RETRIBUTION, AND YOU WANT TO GET IT FROM INSIDE HIS HOUSE. . . .

PRIVATE MOMENTS If you don't live in the same residence as your Target, this one can get you in trouble, so be careful how you use it. You've probably already noticed when you're on an airplane flight that there are usually two magazines in the seat pocket in front of you. One is a catalogue of items you can order through their SkyMall. On one of the pages, you will find an object with a concealed video camera inside. Mostly, these type of hidden cameras are used to see if the nanny or babysitter is doing anything wrong while watching little Junior. If someone had a devious mind, the camera could also be used to commit the Target's embarrassing habits to video. A little something to be used later?

THAT'S RIGHT, BABY DIAPERS   There's a water-absorbent gel, known as sodium salt of polyacrylic acid, in disposable diapers that soaks up moisture when baby hasn't yet been potty trained. As baby's released water hits the gel, the liquid passes through the gel membrane and swells each of these little white beads to a larger size. Now picture these water absorbent beads poured down the drain of your Target's bathroom or kitchen sink. They hit the water in the gooseneck and expand. Drain closes, nothing moves. When the beads dry out, they shrink back to original size, but there always seems to be water in a gooseneck drain. Experiment with the number of diapers you need to come up with a sufficient quantity of gel.

AIRBORNE   Here's one for the ceiling fan over your Target's bed. Vacuum up all the house dust you can find and place it in a container. Turn off the ceiling fan over his bed and get high enough up to reach all the fan blades. Sprinkle fine dust evenly along the topside of each blade. When he gets ready for bed that warm night and turns on the overhead fan, the dust, almost invisible to the naked eye, will gradually spin off of the blades and float down to tickle his sinuses. There's nothing like continuous sneezing for a good night's rest.

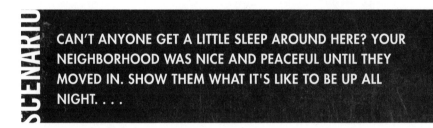

SCENARIO

CAN'T ANYONE GET A LITTLE SLEEP AROUND HERE? YOUR NEIGHBORHOOD WAS NICE AND PEACEFUL UNTIL THEY MOVED IN. SHOW THEM WHAT IT'S LIKE TO BE UP ALL NIGHT. . . .

ALL NIGHT LONG Jiminy Cricket may have been a loveable character in the movie *Pinocchio*, but late-night chirping by a cricket searching for a mate is downright loud and annoying. And, when you get close to a chirping cricket, he knows you're there, so he quits making noise until you leave, which means he's damn hard to find and eradicate. A couple dozen of these ugly bugs inside the Target's house will provide a symphony of discord to sleep

by. And, the nice thing is you don't even have to catch your own, just go down to your local pet shop where they sell live ones for snake food.

THE SHADOW RETURNS Remember lying in bed at night in summertime with the lights out, watching TV, and then something flits past the TV set. You saw the motion, but now it's gone. Then, in a few minutes it comes fluttering back across the front of the TV screen. Now you have to get up and find a fly swatter to kill that crazy moth drawn to the light. But, he's gone again, so you lay back and wait. Yep, here he comes again. Does this help you picture your Target's frustration when he finds several of these little kamikazes he has to keep getting up to swat? Any kind of moth should fit your needs for this situation.

THAT ANNOYING SOUND This is perfect if your Target's bedroom has a ceiling fan. Using your tube of superglue, attach several heavy, metal washers to the top side of one fan blade. The farther outboard you fix them the more unbalanced the movement of the overhead fan, which causes more wobble in its rotation. More wobble means the fan produces an annoying noise, usually a loud click for every rotation. All night long, he hears a *click*, *click*, *click*, until he turns the fan off. In the dog days of summer when it's hot inside, a fan can be a necessity for comfort.

THAT CHEAP BASTARD! YOUR NEXT-DOOR NEIGHBOR WILL NICKEL AND DIME YOU EVERY CHANCE HE GETS, AND THEN WHENEVER THERE'S A TIME WHERE HE OWES YOU MONEY, HE JUST SAYS, "THANKS, BUDDY." GET SOME REVENGE BY SQUEEZING SOME CHANGE OUT OF HIS POCKETS. . . .

THERE'S A LEAK SOMEWHERE This one requires a period of time, several visits to the Target's house, and only works if he has a grill with a propane tank. Observe how his tank is hooked up to the grill just in case you need a wrench. Disconnect the hose and open the valve by turning the handle. Only let out some of the propane. Remember, you will be making several trips to let out small quantities over a period of time. He will believe he has a leaky connection somewhere and keep looking for something that doesn't exist.

WARNING! Do not smoke during this operation.

THE PRICE OF WATER Have you looked at your water bill lately? What used to be free from the nearest stream or well now costs the homeowner big bucks. And, if you're buying bottled water, you're paying more for a gallon of that than you are for a gallon of gas. In any case, water is now expensive, so the next time your Target goes on vacation, or even a three-day weekend, you merely turn on his outside faucet with attached hose and let the dollars flow. By the time he gets home, he'll have a swamp in the back yard and a hefty water bill to pay.

LIGHTS OUT When you do a recon inside your Target's residence, note the brand name and wattages of light bulbs used in his lamps. Go to the store and purchase several bulbs in those brands and wattages. Jar the bulbs enough to break the filament inside each bulb. Now, using a random pattern of the times you are inside the Target's residence, replace his good bulb with your damaged bulb. You end up with a good light bulb, and he starts thinking he's got a lamp with a short in it because the bulbs keep burning out. You'll know your mission succeeded when he buys a new lamp to replace the old one. Hey, you get a free lamp that way too.

YOU'VE HAD IT. YOUR NEIGHBOR'S DOG COMES OVER AND USES YOUR LAWN LIKE IT'S A TOILET. YOU CAN'T STEP ANYWHERE WITHOUT SINKING INTO MUSHY TERDS AND YOUR GRASS IS STARTING TO DIE. TIME TO OWN THAT DOG'S MASTER. . . .

THAT DIRTY SKUNK Spread some skunk scent—bought at your local hunting-supply store—in a camouflage bundle into the Target's yard near the dividing fence line. This way, his neighbor's dog will be the one con-

stantly barking for no apparent reason and the Target will be the recipient of all the noise. Sooner or later, he will either try to do something to the dog, have words with his neighbor, or call the police to report a noise disturbance. Any one of which puts him at odds with his neighbors. Repeat the bundle toss as often as necessary to accomplish the mission.

THE PAVLOV THEORY As an experiment in psychology, Pavlov rang a bell when he fed his dogs. The dogs associated the ringing bell with being fed, so when Pavlov subsequently rang the bell, the dogs salivated as if food was in front of them even though it wasn't. His experiment shows that animals can be trained through association. So, get yourself a miniature poodle, Chihuahua, or other small, cute, innocent-looking dog and train it to hate the person who is your Target. If the dog attacks his ankles, you claim that he must have provoked your pet. Have several previous witnesses as to how gentle and safe your small dog is. Act astounded that the only person your pet attacks is your Target.

 If you're really diabolical and have access to your Target's dog, train it to not like him. Whoa, you say, how do I do this? Admittedly, it takes a certain amount of cruelty on your part. You acquire a large piece of the Target's clothing and use it to tease the animal to the point of rage. The dog will soon associate the Target's scent with anger. After your Target gets attacked and gets rid of the animal, if your conscience bothers you, you can always adopt the dog and put it in therapy to resolve its conflicting emotions. After all, they say a dog is man's best friend.

POOPER SCOOPER So you've got a friend with a very large dog that needs lots of exercise, especially late at night. Borrow the dog and feed it well, preferably something to loosen its bowels. Keep your new-found canine friend on the sidewalk until you get to the Target's grassy lawn. Pause for the dog to get his job done. There's nothing like trying to shovel loose crap out of your grass the next day.

The stink tends to linger well during hot weather. For deniability on your part, carry a plastic bag visible in one hand, so people perceive you as a conscientious person who immediately cleans up his dog's mess. Crap, keep walking.

WHEN NATURE CALLS, LET YOUR A-HOLE NEIGHBOR ANSWER. HE'S DONE ONE TOO MANY THINGS TO PISS YOU OFF AT THIS POINT. YOU MIGHT AS WELL LET MOTHER NATURE GET VENGEANCE FOR YOU. . . .

BIRD POOP Ever walk under a tree where birds gather and then have to watch where you step to keep from getting anything on your shoes? That's roughly the concept we're shooting for here, and you can do this from outside his house.

Frequently scatter grain and bird food in out-of-the way places on his roof. Birds of all kinds, depending upon the type of food you just served them, will gather on his roof to eat. Not only will they make an annoying din, but they will also poop on his house, yard, and vehicles. His roof will look like something out of that Alfred Hitchcock movie *The Birds*.

SOUNDS IN THE ATTIC As you look around your Target's neighborhood for ideas, pay attention to trees near his house, ones with branches growing close to his roof. Watch for the presence of squirrels in the area. If he has both squirrels and tree branches they can use to gain access to his roof, then you're in business. Every so often, toss a few ears of dried corn up on his roof in places where the corn won't be noticeable. Eventually, the squirrels, while enjoying their free lunch, will start gnawing their way into the attic so they can have food and shelter in the same place.

THEY'RE EVERYWHERE Tough to kill off, box elder bugs come back every year to a wood siding they like. In the warm days of autumn, they invade buildings to seek shelter from the coming winter. Attracted to lights, they fly in open doors and windows. Indoors, these bugs are a nuisance, producing a foul odor when crushed, and staining curtains with fecal matter. Outdoors, they cluster in large numbers on trees and buildings. They hide in cracks and crevices in walls, doors, and window casings, around foundations, in stone piles, tree holes, and other protected places. On warm days during winter and early spring, they reappear on light-painted surfaces on the south and west sides of the house, resting in the sun. So collect a few and relocate to the house of your choice.

SCENARIO

YOUR JACKASS NEIGHBOR CONTINUALLY COMMENTS ON YOUR LAWN. ANY TIME YOU WAIT MORE THAN THREE DAYS TO MOW, HE'S STANDING BY YOUR DRIVE-WAY WHEN YOU COME HOME FROM WORK. WAIT UNTIL THE CURMUDGEON GOES AWAY FOR A COUPLE DAYS AND THEN SHOW HIM WHAT A BAD LAWN REALLY LOOKS LIKE. . . .

LAWN GRAFFITI Graffiti artists use cans of spray paint to decorate freight cars, inner-city walls, and bridges, but with a small pump sprayer and a commercial strength mixture of herbicide, you can release some of your more creative talents in a more personal way. Using a herbicide that kills all plant life, not just the weeds, you apply graffiti to your Target's front lawn. Decide whether you want the Target to be able to read it from his front window or if you want the neighbors be able to read it as they pass by. If you are truly artistic, create a line drawing, but don't sign your artwork. Your graffiti remains visible until his newly planted grass grows out to cover it.

TOUCH OF DEATH If you prefer your Target does his own damage to the lawn, swap the contents of his pesticide container with the contents of his herbicide container. Every flower, bush, or tree he sprays to rid it of insects will turn brown and die. And, every weed he sprays to eradicate will suddenly be free of insects gnawing away at its leaves and stalk. True, this method will take longer to have its effect because you are waiting on him to take action, but to some degree, it gives you the anticipation of having a present; you just don't know when the present will be opened.

I GOT NO ROOTS Find some of those cute little white grub worms in your lawn or garden? Since you believe in live and let live, instead of spraying for these voracious eaters of grass and plants, you do the humane thing. Dig them up and relocate them to various parts of your Target's lawn and garden where they continue to reproduce and gnaw away at the roots of his greenery. Let him wonder why his grass turns brown in spots and his plants wither and die. Merely another act of Nature.

 SCENARIO

WHEN THE TARGET IS GONE FOR A FEW DAYS, SNEAK INTO HIS HOUSE AND HAVE SOME FUN INSIDE. . . .

UNHINGED You're in your Target's house and you brought along a hammer, a thin-bladed screwdriver, and a large nail. At every door in the house, you insert the pointed end of the nail into the underside of the door hinge. Use the hammer to drive the hinge pin upward. Place the blade of your screwdriver under the head of the hinge pin to force the pin out. Collect the pins and take them with you. Doors should be closed during this process. Leave pins in whichever door you use as an exit so it stays up. Now, every time the Target opens a door, it keeps on going.

A SCIENCE EXPERIMENT GONE BAD Pull the plug to the refrigerator or freezer. Accelerate the loss of cold temperature inside by holding the refrigerator or freezer door open for a while. Remove all ice cubes in order to help the interior rise to room temp. The resulting mess will be several strains of mold growing up the walls, each mold colony being a different color depending upon the food source. To add confusion to the situation, plug the unit in again before his arrival back home. A variation on this, and less work than pulling the plug, would be to throw the circuit breaker to that unit and reset it later.

THE VALVE FLAPPER THINGY Lift the lid on the toilet tank and locate the chain that raises the valve flap. The valve flap is that circular piece of rubber that gets pulled up to dump water out of the tank, which then flushes the toilet. When the flap comes down again, it stops the water and

allows the tank to fill up again for the next flush. But, when you hook the chain up so the flap can't come down, water just keeps on flowing down the toilet drain, and the water meter keeps on spinning. One man mentioned in the newspapers went on vacation and came home to a four-figure water bill. Ouch.

LOCATION 9

THE
OFFICE

SHAME ON YOU FOR DOING THAT.

Most offices are places where the competition among coworkers is so strong that it becomes a rat race, a matter of survival of the fittest, else be left behind. There's the back-slapping coworker who steals your ideas to get himself advanced over you, the false-face employee bad mouthing you to the boss, and the do-nothing employee on your team who is riding on the group's coattails. You've seen them all and been screwed by them all one way or another. Only Machiavelli would be proud of this group. You're tired and you're not going to take it anymore. Here's some subtle Ways to kick some office butt.

SCENARIO

THAT IT GUY IS GETTING ON YOUR LAST NERVE. ANY TIME YOU HAVE AN ISSUE WITH YOUR COMPUTER, HE TREATS YOU LIKE SOME SORT OF CHILD. MR. COMPUTER WHIZ MESSED WITH THE WRONG PERSON. . . .

BAD MOUSE Sometimes, it's the little annoyances in life that really drag on a person's mental state. You know, those days where everything goes wrong and you should've just stayed in bed until the world got better. Flip his mouse over

and remove three of those four small pads on the bottom, those little slick pads that allow the mouse to glide smoothly over the surface of the desk. The mouse now has resistance to movement and drags in other directions. There goes the ease of moving the cursor where he wants it to go. One more nail in the coffin.

THERE'S ONLY 25 LETTERS IN MY ALPHABET

Turn your Target's computer keyboard face down. Unscrew the back plate. See all the working parts in there? Bend one of those parts or disconnect it so that one key for the alphabet no longer works. It's best if your Target can still get the key on his keyboard to move like it's working when he hits the key but nothing shows up on the screen. Try to pick a letter not frequently used in spelling out words in the English language. You want to frustrate him, but you don't want him to fix the problem too early. It's more fun when he tries to find other words that don't use the corrupted letter of the alphabet that he needs.

POLARIZING HIS CPU You can experiment with this one. Obtain a strong commercial magnet or a handful of small magnets. With a commercial magnet, pass it over the top and along the sides of your Target's CPU. The inner workings of a computer tower are sensitive to static electricity; therefore, a strong magnet will realign how some electronic parts work. With the small magnets, you'll have to open the tower case and place the small magnets in various out-of-sight places inside the case but close to motherboard and driver units. Only use the second method if you're sticking it in his face that someone tampered with his computer.

SCENARIO

MAN, THIS GUY IS GETTING ON YOUR NERVES. EVERY TIME HE COMES TO YOUR DESK, HE HAS SOMETHING CONDESCENDING TO SAY TO YOU. AND AS IF THAT ISN'T BAD ENOUGH, EACH TIME HE STARTS TO BERATE YOU, HE BRINGS HIS GLASSES DOWN THE BRIDGE OF HIS NOSE TO LOOK DOWN ON YOU. . . .

NOW YOU SEE IT, NOW YOU DON'T Locate his second pair, whether they are sunglasses, reading glasses, or even a backup pair. Take out the screws in the hinges and the nosepiece. Lightly file down the threads on all the screws and then reinsert the screws. The next time you get access to the pair of glasses he is currently wearing, do the

same to those screws. Eventually, they will come loose and his frames will fall apart. If you're lucky, this happens when your Target has an important business meeting, and all he has to fix them with is black electrician tape. Nice image to show his peers.

THROUGH A LENS DARKLY Obtain temporary possession of his prescription glasses. Take the glasses to a one-hour service place and ask for a new lens on just one side of the glasses. The new lens to be installed should be one full strength higher than the old lens. Get the glasses back to your Target before he notices. Usually, people with prescription glasses also have prescription sunglasses, so you may be able to work with whichever pair is currently sitting in the glasses case, and do the other pair later. You might also remove all pain reliever medicines, which would alleviate the Target's sudden headaches he's sure to get.

WHERE'D THEY GO? If you know someone with glasses, you know they are *always* losing them. So all you need to do is help your Target out, and pretty soon he'll be losing his mind. Any time he puts his glasses down and steps away from his desk, move his glasses. Don't hide them. Just put them in a different spot on his desk. (Okay, maybe you can hide them *a little*.) Pretty soon you'll hear him cursing himself every time he comes back to his desk. Mission accomplished.

SOME ADVICE...

The game of psychological warfare is a continuing process in which you get to know everything about your opponent before you start to work on his humiliation or destruction. The information you gather allows you to figure out the best way to plan his downfall. It tells you his personal strengths and his weaknesses, his actions and reactions. It gives you the patterns and routines of his life, his likes and his dislikes, his dreams and his fears, the number and depth of his friendships, and the power of his enemies. If the information-gathering process is done correctly, you get to know your Target even better than he knows himself, and you can use it against him.

SCENARIO

SERIOUSLY? HOW DEAF IS THAT KID IN THE CUBICLE OVER THAT HE HAS TO LISTEN TO HIS IPOD THAT LOUD? FORGET TATTLING TO THE BOSS. IT'S TIME TO TAKE ON THIS NUISANCE YOURSELF. . . .

NUKE IT Get your hands on your Target's iPod. Five minutes should be all the time you need. Go directly to the nearest microwave unit. Okay, so you should probably plan this one for a time and place where a microwave is handy, say someone's kitchen or the company break room. Place the iPod in the microwave and nuke for about seven seconds.

There should be sparks coming off of any metal pieces. If there are no sparks or loud crackling noises then add a few seconds to the nuke time. Microwaves are tough on metal. Something in his iPod will now cease to operate as intended. Do not melt the plastic; you don't want him to be able to see that something is wrong.

YOU'RE COMING IN BROKEN Does your Target always have those ear buds stuck in his ears and you can't get his attention for important issues? Does he always seem to be dancing to a different tune when he should be with the program? There is a simple solution. Just glom onto his iPod at some time when he has to set it aside for business or other activities. Crimp the wires for one or both ears back and forth until the wires inside the rubber tubing become broken. His music then becomes intermittent, which is no fun when his favorite song is playing.

IT'S GOING AROUND Forget screwing with his iPod; it's time for some biological warfare. (Hey, if he's ruining your ears, you might as well ruin his body.) Know somebody coming down with a bad cold? Surreptitiously collect some of their saliva or mucus on a tissue while they're still contagious, then apply to the inside and outside of the rim of your Target's current drink glass or coffee mug. Hey, it's not your fault if he gets sick; after all, cold germs are everywhere. Okay, so in this case you know better, but no one else does. You can enjoy his daily suffering through the discomfort of sneezes, coughs, etc. Just stay far enough away from him that you don't get the cold germ too.

KNOW THE LINGO

BIOLOGICAL WARFARE

This is a type of combat that makes use of viruses, toxins, or bacteria to destroy the enemy.

SCENARIO

THE OFFICE SUCK-UP HAS BEEN STEALING YOUR IDEAS AND PASSING THEM OFF AS IF THEY WERE HIS OWN. . . .

LONGFELLOW If you are an aspiring poet, or can at least make a few words rhyme with each other, then put your talents to work. Craft up a few crude, risqué, and amateur poems featuring the Target's opposite-sex boss or coworker and then manage to leave the poems on that person's desk. Have some mention in the poem that subtly refers back to the Target, or which could have supposedly only come from him. Naturally, the pervert himself wouldn't sign such a poem with his real name, so use a nom de plume that reflects one of the Target's obvious physical or personality traits.

WHAT DO YOU MEAN SEXUAL HARASSMENT?

Check with the office gossip so you can choose wisely who to send the gift to. What gift you ask? Why the sexually inappropriate one that arrives on the desk of one of the Target's coworkers. If your Target is ugly, send it to the office beauty queen. If he's good looking, then send it to the happily married woman who is very religious. He can deny all he wants, but there's his name on the return label. Include a suggestive note about how they could meet after hours and use the gift together.

IT HAD TO BE YOU Send a romantic card to the Target's same-sex boss or coworker with no return name or address on the envelope. Acquire a document with the Target's signature on it. Take a piece of transparent paper, place this paper on top of his, signature and carefully trace over the first letter of his first name. You then put the traced initial on top of the card in a position where someone would normally sign his name. Using a ballpoint pen, trace heavily over the initial so it makes a slight impression in the card. Fill in the impression with a felt tip pen. Looks like the Target signed the card with his first initial.

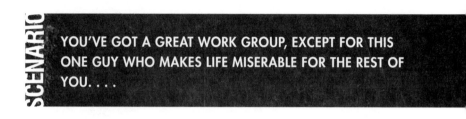

SCENARIO

YOU'VE GOT A GREAT WORK GROUP, EXCEPT FOR THIS ONE GUY WHO MAKES LIFE MISERABLE FOR THE REST OF YOU. . . .

SOMETHING'S ROTTEN IN DENMARK Pick out a sexy female in your workplace or in his and her social group and find out what aftershave, cologne, or shampoo that fem fatale likes a man to use. Then one day in passing conversation you happen to pass this info on to the Target's girlfriend, after which you anonymously mail a bottle of that particular item to him. Later, you casually remark to his girlfriend about the new smell he has. Once a female has the seeds of suspicion sown in her mind, she will find other things about him to bring up in lover's spats.

ANOTHER GREEN-EYED MONSTER If your Target's girlfriend works in the same office, send a balloon bouquet to him at that address. The accompanying card should include a sexy-sounding female name and a few words about getting together later for drinks and who knows what. The more suggestive the card, the better. Pay cash so there's no way to trace the purchase back to your name, and if you can get a female friend to make the purchase, then your story is solid if he checks with the florist as to who sent the bouquet. The girlfriend will never believe he doesn't know a female by that name on the card.

OR TRY THIS! To work the reverse angle on the Way above, have a friend, or you could use an alias, send a dozen roses to the Target's girlfriend at her residence or workplace just before the Target shows up. The attached card should have some sentiment such as, "Thanks for just being you" or "That was a great time we had." Do not put a signature on the card. Even though she doesn't know who sent the flowers, she will be flattered at such attention and yet will resent being put on the defensive by her boyfriend's attitude and accusing questions. Thus, out of beauty comes chaos.

THE 900-POUND GORILLA Want her whole office talking so your Target can't help but hear? Send a singing gorilla to his girlfriend's workplace. By the time the gorilla finishes making her the center of romantic attention with his antics, she's blushing and every tongue in her office is gossiping. She'll ask the Target later if he sent the gorilla. Naturally, he didn't, but where does that leave his peace of mind? He's got to wonder if some rogue male is moving in on his territory. Combine this with other Ways to deepen his newfound insecurity, and when he starts tightening the reins on her, she'll consider him to be a party pooper.

There Was This One Time . . .

Make your opponent think you have the best hand in the game. In a fit of power, a one-star general needlessly embarrassed me in front of coworkers during one of our operations. I contemplated my options and subsequently told his chief of staff that I had prepared a resignation letter to Washington, DC, because I could no longer do the job under the present circumstances, and if I did not get an apology, then the letter was going forward. The general had to consider that the year before I ensured he received a commendation from Washington for one of our previous operations, plus the perception that I was friends with a politician who could affect the general's career. I got my apology and the word spread through the ranks. In reality, the politician connection was all perception, part of my bluff.

YOUR COWORKER IS ONE OF THOSE TYPE OF GUYS WHO STABS YOU IN THE BACK AND THEN ACCUSES YOU OF STEALING THE SILVERWARE. . . .

SNAKE IN THE STALL Your Target is a snake in the grass with the habit of going to the men's room every day about the same time. So, the next time he goes, you are prepared. Quietly bungee cord the stall door shut. Looks like someone is stuck on the pot.

A NEW SLANT ON THE WORLD You'd love to have your obnoxious coworker in an interrogation room, but you're willing to settle for some discomfort on his part. Interrogators want their subject to be uncomfortable. If he is cool, calm, and collected, it is easier for him to lie, but when he is off balance, his mind is partially occupied with whatever is making him uncomfortable, and therefore he cannot fully focus on lying to you. One of the old, subtle Ways is to saw off part of the front legs of the chair he will sit in. This keeps sliding him forward on the seat, which causes him to use leg muscles to stay in position, thus eventually depleting his energy and his will. To avoid easy detection of your handiwork, you should probably only saw off one inch from each of the front legs of his favorite wooden chair or work stool.

STICKY SITUATION Find your Target's file for his next presentation to the group or a reference book he needs for daily office use. Then whenever you have the chance, use glue to stick the pages together. You can glue all the pages or select certain pages according to how much time you have. You can also elect to glue just the top of the page, the outside edges, or the full face of the page. If you want to give the Target some hope of saving the book and yet prolong his efforts, then I recommend gluing the top of one page and the bottom of another in random order.

SCENARIO

YOU'VE GOT A COWORKER WHO CAN'T KEEP HIS HANDS OFF OTHER PEOPLE'S FOOD IN THE BREAK ROOM REFRIGERATOR. EVEN WHEN YOU CLEARLY LABEL YOUR PERSONAL LUNCH AND SNACK CONTAINERS, YOU FIND SOME OF YOUR FOOD AND DRINK ITEMS MISSING, OR WORSE, THERE ARE TEETH MARKS. UGH, THE TEETH MARKS AREN'T YOURS. . . .

RELAX That night, you make up whatever item is the thief's favorite food or drink to steal. Of course, you add laxative, liquid to a liquid and solid laxative to a solid food. Mark the package "keep out," but don't put your name on it.

WARNING! Do not use ipecac syrup as the laxative because it can cause heart problems and should be used only under a doctor's supervision.

THAT'S SOUR MILK Vinegar has several uses for changing the flavor of liquids. For instance, take that fresh jug of milk sitting in your Target's refrigerator. Your Target may like a refreshing glass of cow juice to help kick off his morning wakeup, or maybe he just likes lots of milk on his morning cereal. Well, you can ruin the start of his day by simply inserting some vinegar into that jug of fresh milk, at which time the milk quickly becomes sour and affects the taste of any food it gets poured on. And, since milk sours all the time, this appears to be merely another act of nature.

THE LUSH Does your Target have an affinity for fruits or foods that lend themselves to easy tampering? Let's say your Target likes to eat a couple of oranges during the day. You simply fill a syringe up with vodka and inject this colorless, almost tasteless liquor into his oranges. Spread the vodka evenly throughout the fruit because a strong concentration of alcohol in one area may trigger his taste buds to realize that the orange he just bit into has something extra in it. If his supervisor happens to eat one of these loaded fruits and discovers its secret, he will soon assume that your Target is a lush trying to get away with drinking on the job.

There Was This One Time . . .

A guy over whom I had no direct authority enjoyed harassing the group's secretary. I warned him, but he didn't listen. The next day, I arrived early at his private office. On the inside of his door frame I taped up a flash bulb, loud buzzer, and a battery pack, and ran the wires almost down to the floor. To complete the electrical connection, I drove two nails through a spring-type clothespin and attached one end of the wire to one nail and the other end of the circuit to the other nail. If the clothespin was closed it completed the circuit. I had inserted a small square of plastic between the two nail ends and tied a string to the plastic while taping the other string end to the almost closed door. He opened the door, pulled out the plastic, and *Bang*!

On the second day, I arrived early again. This time, I used a mercury switch to activate my booby trap. You can purchase these at most electronics store. I taped the mercury switch to the back of his office chair, along with my usual flash bulb, loud buzzer, and battery pack. I wired all the components together and turned his chair so that its back faced the wall to keep him from noticing the addition. He came in later and sat in his chair. When he put his feet on the desk and leaned back, the mercury switch tilted enough to complete the circuit, and *Bang*!

On the third day, I used a pressure switch. You can wire these babies to activate the circuit when a weight is placed on the switch or when a weight is removed from the switch. I wired up my usual flash bulb, loud buzzer, and battery pack to the pressure switch. I had held down the top of the switch and placed his favorite magazine on it for weight. The Target soon entered his office and decided to continue reading. As soon as he picked up the magazine, the weight on the switch was removed, the electrical circuit was completed, and *Bang*!

On the fourth day, I didn't bother to come into the office early. And I didn't bother to install any more booby traps. For several hours that day, the Target kept going over all parts of his office looking for the next booby trap. But, you know what, there wasn't one there. His problem was the paranoia in his mind that the next item he turned over, the next action he took, might set off another hidden buzzer and flashbulb. His own paranoia kept him on pins and needles for several days waiting for something that wasn't going to happen. He knew that just because he was paranoid didn't mean someone wasn't out to get him.

SOME ADVICE . . .

In an Associated Press release concerning paranoia, studies by British psychologist Daniel Freeman showed that nearly one-fourth of Londoners has regular thoughts of paranoia, while over 40 percent of the participants in the study had at least some paranoid thoughts. "Paranoia is defined as the exaggerated or unfounded fear that others are trying to hurt you. That includes thoughts that other people are trying to upset or annoy you, for example, by staring, laughing or making unfriendly gestures." Studies by other experts showed that rates of paranoia have recently increased dramatically.

THIS GUY'S CROSSED YOU FOR THE LAST TIME. YOU THOUGHT HE HAD YOUR BACK, BUT THE FIRST CHANCE HE GOT TO THROW YOU UNDER THE BUS, HE TOOK IT. TIME FOR SOME PAYBACK. . . .

PARANOID! Leave your Target little notes saying something to the extent of "I know what you did" followed by "Shame on you for doing that." Continue along that line for several days at random intervals. Create the notes from words cut out of magazines or newspapers and then glue the words on a piece of paper so he can't figure out the handwriting or trace the note back to a particular printer. Everybody has done something they are ashamed of, and while you may not know what it was that your Target did, his mind will run overtime trying to figure out which incident the anonymous person may know about.

SHaME On
Y'll FoR
loinG TbAT.

THE PHOTO With the digital photo software available these days, you don't have to work for the CIA to phony up a photograph. Almost any amateur can do it. So, browse the Internet for cross-dresser sites until you find someone with a build like your obnoxious neighbor. Download or copy the photo. Using a picture of your Target, remove his head and place it on the cross-dresser picture. Post the photo to a website long enough to show your coworkers the picture of him in lingerie. Don't give out the URL for this site. Then erase the photo with no trail for anyone to follow back.

DIRTY BROWSER This one only works if you can figure out your Target's password(s) to get onto his computer and get access to his Internet provider. Look around his desk. People who change their passwords frequently have trouble remembering them, so they write them down somewhere close. Assuming you acquired the password(s), surreptitiously download several hardcore porn sites onto his company computer. Now, disable the computer so your Target needs a repairman. When the serviceman finds the porn, he'll mention it to the company's administrators. The embarrassment begins with his denial. Remember, wear gloves so no fingerprints are left behind. Also, you only want to embarrass your Target, not send him to prison, so don't download any kiddie porn.

THE GREAT
OUTDOORS

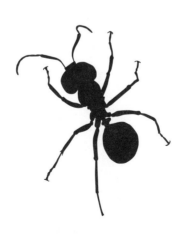

The Great Outdoors has always been a place where a man could challenge the forces of nature, be it steep mountains, adverse weather, wild creatures, or competition with other humans. It tests your physical endurance, your mental perseverance, and your ability to adapt, maybe even to survive in the wilderness. And, along with all the potential activities in the Great Outdoors come potential situations where you can kick your Target's ass. You merely need to figure out what outdoor activities he likes to do or places where he's vulnerable, and you can get at him. Study your opponent and you'll find a Way.

SCENARIO

CAN'T YOU JUST TAKE A HIKE WITHOUT HAVING TO DEAL WITH PEOPLE ZIPPING AROUND ON BIKES—MOTORIZED OR OTHERWISE? TAKE YOUR TARGET (AND HIS RIDE) DOWN, ONE WHEEL AT A TIME. . . .

THE WILD ONE If your Target has a dirt bike, a highway cruiser, or a chopper, all you need is the right-sized socket and a ratchet. By applying the ratchet and socket to the bolt that locks down the handlebars, you loosen the bolt enough

to twist them a few degrees out of alignment. Don't twist so far as to be visibly noticeable. Retighten the bolt. On a long ride, your Target will start to feel fatigue in one arm but not know why. The bike will also handle differently in the curves, Just enough to throw off his day. About the time his mind and body start to adapt to the change, loosen the bolt and turn the handlebars a few degrees in the opposite direction.

THE CYCLE OF LIFE You're in a bicycle race involving your Target as one of the competitors and you want to wreck him on the course. Do not use your front wheel to run into his rear wheel. All that will do is cause you to lose control of your own bicycle, and down you go. A better scenario involves having a few sturdy tree branches about pencil thick and nine to twelve inches in length eas-ily available to your hand nearest his bicycle. Ride next to his rear tire and surreptitiously toss sticks, one at a time, to place them into the spokes of his rear wheel. When a stick jams between the spokes and the bike frame, his abrupt stop becomes fall-down mode.

THE SUDDEN UNICYCLE If your Target likes to ride a bicycle on rough terrain, all you need to help him out is a crescent wrench and a couple of uninterrupted minutes to play mechanic. Use the crescent wrench to loosen the axle nuts on both sides of his front wheel. Don't loosen the nuts so far that it's easily noticeable to the naked eye, only enough so that when he hits the next big bump, his front wheel will separate from the front bicycle fork. His two-wheeled vehicle has now become a unicycle. By the way, just how good are his reflexes?

There Was This One Time . . .

There are also psychological Ways to kick someone's ass. Some of these take advance preparation and others are Targets of opportunity, such as the helicopter pilot, to remain nameless, who claimed to be tough enough to take a punch. Being in a bar, his associates plied him with liquor while professing their admiration for his alleged toughness. When he was suitably drunk, one of the associates made a doubting remark, whereupon the pilot, to prove his point, let himself be talked into having a bystander punch him. Knocked off his bar stool, the pilot immediately jumped up, saying he wasn't hurt. The bystander, one of the associates' conspirators, stated it wasn't his best punch. The cycle continued for a while. Thus, you see how to get a fool to kick his own ass if you take the time to set it up right.

MAN, THAT GUY'S A REAL JACKASS. YOU CAN SHOW
HIM. PLAY INTO HIS DELUSIONS OF BEING SOME SORT OF
BADASS AND HAVE HIM KICK HIS OWN ASS. . . .

HEY MAN, IT'S FOR TV TV stations are always showing photo clips of outrageous stunts, plus several networks
pay money for amateur videos. Have a party where lots
of these stunts are shown, discussed, and laughed at, and
then talk your Target into making a video for TV. Tell him
you'll split the money. Of course, he may need it later for
bandages and liniment to sooth his aching body. The more
outrageous the action you talk him into, the better. And,
even if he comes through unscathed this time, you'll have
a movie you can laugh at for years because you tricked him
into doing something stupid. If his first stunt was success-
ful, it should be easy to talk him into an even stupider second video.

BULL-ONEY To continue with
the psychological game of getting
a macho fool to kick his own ass,
head to one of those wild buffalo
farms or a farm that has a bull.
Arrange circumstances so the
Target takes the first ride. Make

sure that he consumes copious quantities of alcohol just before the ride to give him what's known as "liquid courage." Afterward, look at him on the stretcher and say something to the effect of, "I don't know, after what happened to you, that looks too dangerous. Me and the boys decided to take a pass, but you, you sure were brave to ride that crazy monster." Get out of hearing distance before you start laughing.

KNOW THE LINGO

LIQUID COURAGE
The confidence one receives from consuming inebriating beverages.

THAT DIRTY SKUNK From a hunting catalogue, or your local sporting goods store, purchase a small vial of skunk scent. (I know they sell it because a retired Special Forces guy I did some work with in the deep woods used the scent on our water and food caches to keep other animals out.) Take the labeling off the vial. Now tell your Target that it contains an all-natural insect repellent. Just be sure you're not sharing the same tent that night, as he'll be having some visitors.

SOME ADVICE . . .

Everybody has nightmares brought on by the subconscious mind. It could be something out of their past, something currently looming large in their present, something from a movie or a book, all in conjunction with what they fear in the real world. The mind is a tricky mechanism that sometimes works for the person and sometimes against them. And when it goes bad, the mind is very hard to control. So, figure out how to get a piece of your Target's mind. What does he fear more than anything? What gives him the cold sweats? Now you can destroy his peace of mind by working on his fears.

SCENARIO

YOUR JERK OF A "FRIEND" CALLS YOU OUT IN FRONT OF A GROUP OF YOUR PALS ABOUT BEING AFRAID OF SNAKES. AND HE WON'T GIVE IT UP. SHOW HIM TWO CAN PLAY AT THIS GAME. USE YOUR KNOWLEDGE OF HIS ACROPHOBIA TO YOUR ADVANTAGE. . . .

AN ELECTRIFYING EXPERIENCE In the Rocky Mountains of Colorado, there are several mountain peaks known as the "fourteeners" because each peak reaches a height of 14,000 feet or more. For a sense of personal accomplishment, many people hike as many of these as they can. Challenge your Target to hike these peaks during the summer months, but delay the start of your uphill walk until late morning. Somewhere around noon, you fake tiredness or light injury. Encourage your Target to continue to the top. Now, get off the mountain, because lightning storms usually start in the afternoon on those high peaks, and every year some late hiker gets a jolt. Unfortunately, if he gets a lethal charge, he won't be around for you to enjoy his misery.

KNOW THE LINGO

ACROPHOBIA
The fear of heights.

CHICKEN BOY Buy him a ticket to go bungee jumping and give it to him in front of his friends just so you can watch him chicken out. To complete his chicken-out scene, have a friend of yours present who will take the jump to show him up. In short, find his fear, find the appropriate activity, and use it to embarrass him.

HOW HIGH UP IS THIS? If you live near the ocean or have an abandoned rock quarry where locals sneak off for a swim, then you're in luck. While partying near the water, start a conversation about how brave those cliff divers are down in Mexico, but you bet you guys could do it, too. From the water's edge, the proposed jump doesn't look too bad. It's when you get to the top of the cliff that the distance appears greater. Once again, rely on the properties of liquid courage to prompt your Target to take the leap. Have an EMT standing by in case he belly flops.

YOU THOUGHT CAMPING WAS SUPPOSED TO BE FUN — A PEACEFUL TIME IN THE WOODS WITH YOUR FRIENDS WHERE YOU COULD RELAX AND ENJOY NATURE. THEN SOME A-HOLE AND HIS FRIENDS LANDED IN THE CAMPSITE NEXT TO YOURS. . . .

SMELL THAT? Purchase a catch-and-release animal trap. It's a rectangular metal cage that has a weight-activated floor to shut the trap door. Find an area frequented by skunks and bait the trap with their favorite food. The trap should be large enough to catch a skunk, but small enough to keep him from turning around inside. That way he won't spray you when you pick up the cage. Wear gloves and old clothes. Release the skunk into your Target's tent. Open the cage with a long rope, because the skunk can now turn around and spray.

LOOK AT THOSE TEETH Another fun animal is a possum. These are smelly creatures with sharp, pointed teeth, a long nose, and sharp claws. Fortunately for you, the same size and type of cage trap you used for the skunk is also perfect for possums. Bait the trap with overripe bananas. Don't know where possums learned to eat bananas, but they work. Again, release the beast in your Target's campsite where it will root anything they left out in the open before taking to the woods.

BEAR WITH ME Your Target is in the great outdoors, feeling macho like Daniel Boone or the Last of the Mohicans. He's done all the manly camping things and now he's tired. The sun's gone down and he's crawled into his sleeping bag inside the tent. You stayed up to contemplate the stars.

But first, you leave a nice portion of overripe fruit or meat at the foot of his tent opening. It's called bear bait. When the bear shows up, you scream "Bear" as loud as you can. He makes a new door in the other end of his tent. You just saved his life, and now he owes you. Have your fastest sneakers on in case the bear gets ticked at you for ruining his meal.

KNOW THE LINGO

BEAR BAIT
Any concoction created to lure a bear out of the woods and into an intended area.

YOU'RE STUCK WITH AN OBNOXIOUS ROOMMATE DURING A HUNTING EXPEDITION. SOMEHOW YOU WIND UP BUNKING IN A TWO-MAN CABIN WITH THIS FRIEND OF A FRIEND OF A FRIEND. THE WAY IT'S GOING, YOUR WHOLE TRIP WILL BE MORE STRESSFUL THAN IF YOU'D STAYED AT WORK WITH YOUR DICTATORIAL BOSS. TIME TO FIX IT. . . .

CHEESE IT You can trap rats or mice for your get-even project. Just slip the little rodents inside his sleeping bag. I suggest obtaining the brown or gray wild ones as opposed to the gentle kind you can buy in a pet store. Obviously, a white rat running around inside the Target's sleeping bag says that someone put him there, but a brown or gray mouse isn't suspicious because he could have found his own way inside. Scatter cheese around his bed to keep the mice from scurrying too far.

THE STING When disturbed, red ants and fire ants swarm all over their victims, leaving nice red welts on a human's skin. The resulting bites sting for a while. So get yourself one of those cute little clear plastic ant farm containers that kids use for the more tame species. Bait the farm with sugar and place it near

an active red ant colony. After ants have entered the container—the amount you gather depends on how obnoxious your Target really is—close it up tight and boogey before you get bit. You can now plant the container inside your Target's bed, open the lid, and depart the area.

IN HOT WATER You're hot over the situation you find yourself in, and you'd like for your bothersome roommate to feel some of that heat. So, get up real early and take your morning shower. On your way out of the cabin, turn the dial on the hot-water heater all the way up to maximum temperature. Turn off the cold-water source to the shower, or superglue the cold-water handle so it doesn't move. His next shower before heading to breakfast will definitely have him feeling your heat.

OR TRY THIS! Here's the flip side to the hot-water method. On your way out, turn the dial on the hot-water heater all the way down to the "vacation" setting and superglue it in place. Your roommate's next shower becomes an icy blast of how you really feel about him.

DEBRIEFING

When organizations run into trouble, they conduct brainstorming sessions to come up with ways to get around the particular roadblock. In these sessions, anyone with a potential solution speaks his mind. There are no wrong answers. Ideas beget other ideas and spark the brainstormer's creativity until the best possible solution is devised.

This book works the same way.

These Ways are meant to spark your creativity so that when the time comes for you to kick ass, you can use the best possible option to defeat your current roadblock. Whether the particular situation you're in requires an immediate physical reaction or allows time for a more planned-out response, you're now equipped with more than 200 ideas on how to make your Target pay. And like a brainstorming session, you're welcome—even encouraged—to build on the ideas put forth.

The main thing to take away from this exercise in kicking ass is an ability to stand up for yourself. Don't be afraid. Yes, you may get knocked down, but it's not as bad as being walked all over. You have every right to live your life without some jerk telling you differently. Be confident. Violence is not always the answer, but sometimes it's the best solution for taking a stand.

And on top of being smart, be safe. Just as quickly as you could use your hands to deliver an Uppercut or your foot for a Roundhouse, you could use your head and walk away. It's important to learn how to use these maneuvers; it's also important to learn when to use them. While you want plenty of badass stories to tell, you want to be alive to say, *"There was this one time . . . ."*

ABOUT THE AUTHOR

E. R. Silverman is an alias used by the author when he worked undercover for one of those three-letter agencies run by the U.S. government. For twenty-five years, he carried a concealed weapon and has seen his share of violence. Currently, his other writing credits are over sixty published short stories, included in such publications as *Easyriders Magazine* and *Outlaw Biker*, plus several articles.

ART CREDITS